Robert Burns

Selected Poems

Edited by Kenneth Brown

Series Editor: Judith Baxter

D1234108

CAMBRIDGE
UNIVERSITY PRESS

PUBLISHED BY THE PRESS SYNDICATE OF THE UNIVERSITY OF CAMBRIDGE
The Pitt Building, Trumpington Street, Cambridge CB2 1RP, United Kingdom

CAMBRIDGE UNIVERSITY PRESS
The Edinburgh Building, Cambridge CB2 2RU, United Kingdom
40 West 20th Street, New York, NY 10011-4211, USA
10 Stamford Road, Oakleigh, Melbourne 3166, Australia

This edition first published 1998

Printed in the United Kingdom by Scotprint Ltd, Musselburgh, Scotland

Typeset in Sabon and Meta

A catalogue record for this book is available from the British Library

ISBN 0 521 62683 8 paperback

Prepared for publication by Stenton Associates

.

CONTENTS

CAMBRIDGE LITERATURE

This edition of poems by Robert Burns is part of the Cambridge Literature series, and has been specially prepared for students in schools and colleges who are studying these poets as part of their literature course.

This study edition invites you to think about what happens when you read a poem, and it suggests that you are not passively responding to words on the page which have only one agreed interpretation, but that you are actively exploring and making *new* sense of what you read. Your 'reading' will partly stem from you as an individual, from your own experiences and point of view, and to this extent your interpretation will be distinctively your own. But your reading will also stem from the fact that you belong to a culture and a community, rooted in a particular time and place. So, your understanding may have much in common with that of others in your class or study group.

There is a parallel between the way you read these poems and the way they were written. The Resource Notes are devised to help you to investigate the complex nature of the writing process. This begins with the poet's first, tentative ideas and sources of inspiration, moves through to the stages of writing, production and publication, and ends with the text's reception by the reading public, reviewers, critics and students. So the general approach to study focuses on five key questions:

Who has written these poems and why?

What type of texts are these poems?

How were the poems produced?

How do these poets present their subjects?

Who reads these poems? How do they interpret them?

The poems are presented complete and uninterrupted. Unfamiliar words and ideas are explained in the commentary.

The Resource Notes encourage you to take an active and imaginative approach to studying poetry both in and out of the classroom. As well as providing you with information about many aspects of Robert Burns, they offer a wide choice of activities to work on individually, or in groups. Above all, they give you the chance to explore this fascinating collection in a variety of ways: as a reader, an actor, a researcher, a critic, and a writer.

Judith Baxter

INTRODUCTION

'Will the real Robert Burns please stand up?' If twenty different people were each to conjure up the spirit of Robert Burns they might each create a different image and each be justified. He was a most fascinatingly self-contradictory person and has given scope to a wide variety of interpretations of his life and work. Male chauvinist pig or worshipper of the fair sex? Fornicator or romantic lover? Egalitarian or toady and place-seeker? Devout church-goer or pagan anarchist? Simple ploughman poet or well-read literary artist? Drunkard or good companion? Scotland's national Bard or universal poet? Scottish nationalist or British unionist? Jacobite or Hanoverian? Of course you have heard of a poet donning a *persona* or mask to assume a role in which to write a poem, but Burns's masks are so various that you may well say in his case, '*This* is ridiculous!' So is he to be condemned as a hypocrite, or praised as a Protean genius? All these things have been said of him. Or is he simply intoxicated with words, carried away by his own command of the language and of his technique?

Burns had contrary emotional impulses at different times, as we all do, but perhaps he gave his freer rein. He changed, or had to dissemble, his social and political attitudes at different times, as many people have done under a harsh government. He also had a natural dramatic talent which might have borne another kind of fruit had he lived longer.

Through all his performances we can see the constant features which have endeared him to readers the world over: his vivid depiction of relations between the sexes, his love of warm friendship, his amusement at all kinds of human frailty, his hatred of narrow-mindedness, his impatience with convention, his impulsive enjoyment of the pleasures of the moment, his love of a good tune and lively words, his proper pride and his insistence on the basic equality of all human beings.

Why should you be interested in reading the works of a poet who writes in this unfamiliar form of language? Mainly for his artistic qualities: his mastery of scathing satire, of humorous narrative, of rousing or gentle lyrics, of urbane and warm-hearted familiar verse. He is also one of the greatest representatives of a sister literary culture to English, the Scots literary tradition – as worthy of study as the American, or French or German. The language is not as difficult as you might think at first glance, certainly no more difficult than Chaucer. Many words can be recognised as Scottish equivalents of English ones. The solution to other difficulties is to use the facing glossary in this edition.

The language itself can be a good reason for studying Burns. His work represents the creation of a body of literature in a form of language already deserted by the social and intellectual leaders of his nation. Yet this increasingly neglected language was the inheritor of the Scottish nation's self-awareness and of a rich literary tradition. Burns exploits this situation by using a sliding scale of degrees of dialect, from Scottish Standard English at one end, to words used only in his own locality at the other: an example of how literature can be enriched by the use of a wide variety of levels of language. He is the most famous example of a world-class writer from the Anglo-Saxon family of languages who does not use Standard English – an interesting phenomenon.

Kenneth Brown
Department of Language Education
Faculty of Education
University of Strathclyde

Notes on 'Holy Willie's Prayer'

Background

William Fisher was an elder in Burns's parish. Willie took a leading part in bringing an action in the Kirk Session against Gavin Hamilton, Burns's landlord and friend. The charge was, amongst other things, that Hamilton had absented himself from church without excuse, that he had made a journey on a Sunday and that he had neglected family worship. The penalty was excommunication. The parish minister, the Rev Mr Auld, was an ally of 'Holy Willie'. The matter was taken to the Presbytery of Ayr where Hamilton's case was argued and won by a lawyer, Robert Aiken, another friend of the poet. Burns circulated the poem in manuscript in Mauchline, his local village.

You can read a description of the Church of Scotland on page 164.

Verse form

Standard Habbie (see page 180).

Pope: Alexander Pope (1688–1744), one of the great satirical poets of the earlier 18th century in England

Elder: an elected official in presbyterian churches

a sessional process: a legal action in the kirk session, which rules over a parish

Presbytery: a higher court of the presbyterian church

3 *Sends ane to Heaven:* The doctrine of Predestination states that God decides to damn or save souls as He creates them. Willie believes he is saved and no action of his can change that.

8 *left in night:* damned

Holy Willie's Prayer

And send the Godly in a pet to pray.

Pope

Argument

Holy Willie was a rather oldish batchelor Elder in the parish of
Mauchline [Ayrshire], & much & justly famed for that polemical
chattering which ends in tippling Orthodoxy, & for that
Spiritualized Bawdry which refines to Liquorish Devotion. — In a
Sessional process with a gentleman in Mauchline, a Mr Gavin
Hamilton, Holy Willie, & his priest, father Auld, after full
hearing in the Presbytery of Ayr, came off but second best; owing
partly to the oratorical powers of Mr Robt Aiken, Mr Hamilton's
Counsel; but chiefly to Mr Hamilton's being one of the most
irreproachable & truly respectable characters in the country. —
On losing his Process, the Muse overheard him at his devotions as
follows —

O Thou that in the Heavens does dwell,
Wha, as it pleases best Thysel,
Sends ane to Heaven an' ten to Hell
                    A' for Thy glory,
And no for onie guid or ill   5
                    They've done before Thee!

I bless and praise Thy matchless might,
When thousands Thou hast left in night,
That I am here before Thy sight,
                    For gifts an' grace   10
A burning and a shining light
                    To a' this place.

13 *generation:* ancestry

14 *sic:* such

17 *Sax thousand years:* Bishop Ussher (1581–1656) used the genealogical lists in the Bible to calculate the date of the creation of Adam and concluded that it had happened in 4004 BC.

18 *Adam's cause:* Adam committed the first sin against the law of God by eating the fruit of the Tree of the Knowledge of Good and Evil in the Garden of Eden. Since then all his descendants have been sinful by nature. This is known as The Fall of Man.

20 *hell:* Many Christians thought of Hell in mainly physical terms – a place of torture for the wicked after death.

21 *gooms:* gums

25 *chosen:* Willie believes that he was predestined by God at his birth to go to Heaven as one of the Elect, the chosen ones.

26 *grace:* special favour shown by God

27 *a pillar o' Thy temple:* This echoes Revelation 3, verse 12. People of Willie's type larded their conversation with phrases from the Bible. Some of the other Bible passages echoed in Willie's words are at St John's Gospel 5, verse 35; St Matthew's Gospel 13, verse 42; 2nd Corinthians 12, verse 7; Deuteronomy 28, verse 17; Psalm 84, verse 2; Isaiah 52, verse 10. Can you find the connections in Willie's prayer?

32 *fash'd:* troubled

37 *yestreen:* yesterday evening
kens: knowest

39 *be a living plague:* be a constant public disgrace

41 *lift a lawless leg:* break the law of God by having sex outside marriage

What was I, or my generation,
That I should get sic exaltation?
I, wha deserv'd most just damnation   15
              For broken laws
Sax thousand years ere my creation,
              Thro' Adam's cause!

When from my mither's womb I fell,
Thou might hae plung'd me deep in hell   20
To gnash my gooms, and weep, and wail
              In burning lakes,
Whare damnèd devils roar and yell,
              Chain'd to their stakes.

Yet I am here, a chosen sample,   25
To show Thy grace is great and ample:
I'm here, a pillar o' Thy temple,
              Strong as a rock,
A guide, a ruler, and example
              To a' Thy flock!   30

But yet, O Lord! confess I must:
At times I'm fash'd wi' fleshly lust;
An' sometimes, too, in warldly trust,
              Vile self gets in;
But Thou remembers we are dust,   35
              Defiled wi' sin.

O Lord! yestreen, Thou kens, wi' Meg—
Thy pardon I sincerely beg—
O, may't ne'er be a living plague
              To my dishonour!   40
An' I'll ne'er lift a lawless leg
              Again upon her.

44 *Leezie's lass:*   a servant girl in Leezie's household

45 *fou:*   drunk

48 *Wad never steer her:*   would never meddle with her

49–54 Work out Willie's argument for using his religion to reconcile himself to his lust.

55 *chosen:*   the few chosen by God to be saved: the Elect, in Calvinist terminology

56 *chosen race:*   The Children of Israel (the Jews) were chosen by God to be his particular people in the Old Testament. Christians sometimes thought of themselves as successors to the Jews as God's chosen people. The more extreme Scottish presbyterians were particularly given to this way of thinking.

61 *Gau'n Hamilton:*   Gavin Hamilton (1751–1805). See *Background* to this poem.

62 *cartes:*   cards

65 *God's ain Priest:*   Rev Mr Auld

67 *we chasten'd him:*   This refers to the action against Gavin Hamilton in the Mauchline Kirk Session. Work out Willie's version of events.

68 *splore:*   disturbance

72 *potatoes:*   Burns probably chose particularly to have Willy mention Gavin Hamilton's potatoes because one of the charges against Hamilton was that he had required his servants to dig potatoes on a Sunday.

Besides, I farther maun avow—
Wi' Leezie's lass, three times, I trow—
But, Lord, that Friday I was fou,   45
        When I cam near her,
Or else, Thou kens, Thy servant true
        Wad never steer her.

Maybe Thou lets this fleshly thorn
Buffet Thy servant e'en and morn,   50
Lest he owre proud and high should turn
        That he's sae gifted:
If sae, Thy han' maun e'en be borne
        Until Thou lift it.

Lord, bless Thy chosen in this place,   55
For here Thou has a chosen race!
But God confound their stubborn face
        An' blast their name,
Wha bring Thy elders to disgrace
        An' open shame!   60

Lord, mind Gau'n Hamilton's deserts:
He drinks, an' swears, an' plays at cartes,
Yet has sae monie takin arts
        Wi' great and sma',
Frae God's ain Priest the people's hearts   65
        He steals awa.

And when we chasten'd him therefore,
Thou kens how he bred sic a splore,
And set the warld in a roar
        O' laughin at us: 70
Curse Thou his basket and his store,
        Kail an' potatoes!

77 *dinna:* do not
79 *Aiken:* See *Background* and Burns's Argument. Robert Aiken is also the dedicatee of 'The Cotter's Saturday Night', page 41.
83 *hingin:* hanging
snakin: sneering
92 *mercies:* undeserved gifts
93 *gear:* wealth

✦ *Activities*

1 From the following list write down the characteristics that you think Willie possesses:

- pride
- a sense of proportion
- a sense of justice
- religious reverence
- spitefulness
- other-worldliness
- self-centredness
- complacency
- a sense of guilt
- a fear of public opinion
- concern with material gain
- hypocrisy
- self-deception
- small-mindedness
- faith

Write a character sketch of Willie.

2 Consider the impression Willie intends to make on God by using so many phrases from the Bible. Now look for any phrases from the poem which you think are small-minded or vulgar. Write a note about how Burns's command of a variety of styles enables him to create Willie's character.

3 One person speaks uninterrupted throughout this poem. Try reading it aloud with appropriate changes of tone. Discuss why you think the tone of voice should change.

4 Imagine that Willie Fisher has got hold of one of the handwritten copies of this poem circulating in Mauchline. He meets Burns by chance in a country lane. Narrate this incident as if it was an extract from a novel, complete with dialogue. (To be interesting, this must be more than a slanging match.)

Lord, hear my earnest cry and pray'r
Against that Presbyt'ry of Ayr!
Thy strong right hand, Lord, mak it bare   75
         Upo' their heads!
Lord, visit them, an' dinna spare,
         For their misdeeds!

O Lord, my God! that glib-tongu'd Aiken,
My vera heart and flesh are quakin   80
To think how we stood sweatin, shakin,
         An' pish'd wi' dread,
While he, wi' hingin lip an' snakin,
         Held up his head.

Lord, in Thy day o' vengeance try him!   85
Lord, visit him wha did employ him!
And pass not in Thy mercy by them,
         Nor hear their pray'r,
But for Thy people's sake destroy them,
         An' dinna spare!   90

But, Lord, remember me and mine
Wi' mercies temporal and divine,
That I for grace an' gear may shine
         Excell'd by nane;
And a' the glory shall be Thine—   95
         Amen, Amen!

Notes on 'A Poet's Welcome to his love-begotten Daughter; the first instance that entitled him to the venerable appellation of Father'

Background
The birth was on 22nd May, 1785, and the mother was Betty Paton, a servant lass employed by Burns's mother. Burns and Bess must have appeared on the stool of repentance at Sunday service in church and been reproved by the minister for fornication. Burns must have also paid a fine to the church. The baby was brought up by Burns's mother and he made financial provision for her care when he was planning to emigrate to Jamaica in 1786. Burns himself referred to this poem as the 'Welcome to his Bastart Wean'.

Verse form
Standard Habbie (see page 180).

---

1 *wean:* child
Mishanter: bad luck
fa': befall
6 *Tyta:* dada
8 *kintra clatter:* country chatter
9 *kend:* known
10 *clash:* gossip
11 *feckless:* worthless
12 *fash:* bother
16 *kirk and queir:* church and choir
17 *ye're no unwrought for:* You weren't obtained without hard work. Can you pick out later phrases echoing the same thought?
20 *daut:* pet
23 *get:* beget

A Poet's Welcome to his love-begotten Daughter; the first instance that entitled him to the venerable appellation of Father

Thou's welcome, wean! Mishanter fa' me,
If thoughts o' thee or yet thy mammie
Shall ever daunton me or awe me,
      My sweet, wee lady,
Or if I blush when thou shalt ca' me   5
      Tyta or daddie!

What tho' they ca' me fornicator,
An' tease my name in kintra clatter?
The mair they talk, I'm kend the better;
      E'en let them clash!   10
An auld wife's tongue's a feckless matter
      To gie ane fash.

Welcome, my bonie, sweet, wee dochter!
Tho' ye come here a wee unsought for,
And tho' your comin I hae fought for,   15
      Baith kirk and queir;
Yet, by my faith, ye're no unwrought for—
      That I shall swear!

Wee image o' my bonie Betty,
As fatherly I kiss and daut thee,   20
As dear and near my heart I set thee,
      Wi' as guid will,
As a' the priests had seen me get thee
      That's out o' Hell.

25 *dint:*   occasion or thrust
26 *funny:*   merry
　　tint: lost
27 *warl':*   world
　　asklent: awry
29 *plack:*   copper
　　's be: shall be
31 *waur:*   worse
　　bestead: provided
32 *Thou's be as braw and bienly:*   You'll be as finely and warmly.
36 *station:*   rank
41 *heir:*   inherit
42 *stocket mailins:*   livestock and a farm
44 *gie:*   give
46 See *Background* (page 16).

✦ *Activities*

1　This was Burns's first illegitimate child. Trace his attitudes and feelings towards the disapproving community, sexual pleasure, his new daughter, the baby's mother, the fine and the public penance. Discuss the mood that emerges when you put all these together.

2　Form pairs and experiment with reading this poem to each other. Discuss the differences between your ways of reading.

3　You are Gilbert Burns, Robert's younger brother by a year, kindly, loyal, but conventional by nature. Write a letter to your cousin James, a lawyer in distant Montrose, sending him a copy of this poem and giving him your comments on Robert's conduct and the attitude of mind this poem reveals.

Sweet fruit o' monie a merry dint,   25
My funny toil is no a' tint:
Tho' thou cam to the warl' asklent,
            Which fools may scoff at,
In my last plack thy part's be in 't
            The better half o't.   30

Tho' I should be the waur bestead,
Thou's be as braw and bienly clad,
And thy young years as nicely bred
            Wi' education,
As onie brat o' wedlock's bed   35
            In a' thy station.

Lord grant that thou may ay inherit
Thy mither's looks an' gracefu' merit,
An' thy poor, worthless daddie's spirit
            Without his failins!   40
'Twill please me mair to see thee heir it
            Than stocket mailins.

And if thou be what I wad hae thee,
An' tak the counsel I shall gie thee,
I'll never rue my trouble wi' thee—   45
            The cost nor shame o't—
But be a loving father to thee,
            And brag the name o't.

Notes on 'To A Louse'

Background
A louse is a biting parasite believed to infest people who live in dirty conditions.

Verse form
Standard Habbie (see page 180).

---

  1 *gaun:* going
       crowlin: crawling
       ferlie: wonder
  3 *strunt:* strut
  6 *sic:* such
  7 *wonner:* wonder
  8 *saunt:* saint
  9 *fit:* foot
 13 *Swith!:* Off!
       hauffet: temple (of the head)
       squattle: squat
13–18 Do these lines express merely disgust or do you detect some other feeling as well?
 14 *sprattle:* scramble
 15 *cattle:* beasts
 17 *horn nor bane:* combs made of horn or bone
 18 *plantations:* colonies
 19 *haud:* keep
 20 *fatt'rils:* falderals
 21 *Na, faith ye yet!:* Curse you still.

To A Louse,
On Seeing one on a Lady's Bonnet at Church

Ha! whare ye gaun, ye crowlin ferlie?
Your impudence protects you sairly,
I canna say but ye strunt rarely
        Owre gauze and lace,
Tho' faith! I fear ye dine but sparely   5
        On sic a place.

Ye ugly, creepin, blastit wonner,
Detested, shunn'd by saunt an' sinner,
How daur ye set your fit upon her —
        Sae fine a lady!   10
Gae somewhere else and seek your dinner
        On some poor body.

Swith! in some beggar's hauffet squattle:
There ye may creep, and sprawl, and sprattle,
Wi' ither kindred, jumping cattle,   15
        In shoals and nations;
Whare horn nor bane ne'er daur unsettle
        Your thick plantations.

Now haud you there! ye're out o' sight,
Below the fatt'rils, snug an' tight;   20
Na, faith ye yet! ye'll no be right,
        Till ye've got on it —
The vera tapmost, tow'ring height
        O' Miss's bonnet.

26 *grozet:* gooseberry
27 *rozet:* rosin
28 *fell:* deadly
   smeddum: powder
30 *droddum:* backside
31 *wad na been:* would not have been
32 *flainen toy:* flannel cap
33 *aiblins:* perhaps
   bit duddie: small ragged
34 *wyliecoat:* flannel vest
35 *Lunardi:* a balloon-shaped bonnet, the latest fashion
   in 1785
37 *Jenny:* What does the use of the lady's first name tell
   you about her social position?
38 *a' abread:* on display
40 *blastie:* cursed little creature
41 *Thae:* those
47 *gait:* manner

◆ *Activities*

1 What tone does Burns immediately set by his title: 'To a Louse'? (See the description of the traditional ode on page 170.)

2 Pick out all the ironical expressions in the poem. Work out what Burns implies by each of them.

3a Write two or three stanzas in imitation of Burns's poem. You might base your ideas on someone you know and his or her pet. Or you could choose some aspect of modern behaviour that you find ridiculous. You will find details of the Standard Habbie stanza form on page 180.

Or:

b Write a letter to the editor of a tabloid newspaper describing a short incident from modern life which illustrates how some people put on false airs.

My sooth! right bauld ye set your nose out,   25
As plump an' grey as onie grozet:
O for some rank, mercurial rozet,
               Or fell, red smeddum,
I'd gie ye sic a hearty dose o't,
               Wad dress your droddum!   30

I wad na been surpris'd to spy
You on an auld wife's flainen toy;
Or aiblins some bit duddie boy,
               On's wyliecoat;
But Miss's fine Lunardi! fye!   35
               How daur ye do't?

O Jenny, dinna toss your head,
An' set your beauties a' abread!
Ye little ken what cursèd speed
               The blastie's makin!   40
Thae winks an' finger-ends, I dread,
               Are notice takin!

O wad some Power the giftie gie us
To see oursels as ithers see us!
It wad frae monie a blunder free us,   45
               An' foolish notion:
What airs in dress an' gait wad lea'e us,
               An' ev'n devotion!

Notes on 'To A Mouse'

Background
Burns was farming at Mossgiel, near Mauchline, where he had moved with his brother Gilbert after the death of their father and the failure of the family farm at Lochlea. In their first year at Mossgiel they had lost half their crops and so might well have feared that their tenancy would soon come to an end. In October, their younger brother, John, had died at the age of 14.

Verse form
Standard Habbie (see page 180).

---

1 *sleekit:* glossy coated

4 *bickering brattle:* hasty scamper

5 *laith:* loath

6 *pattle:* a staff used for clearing stones from between the two cutting edges of an old type of plough

7 *man's dominion:* See the Bible, Genesis 1, verse 28.

13 *whyles:* sometimes

15 *A daimen icker in a thrave:* an odd ear in twenty-four sheaves

17 *the lave:* what's left

20 *silly:* feeble

21 *big:* build

22 *foggage:* moss

24 *snell:* biting

To A Mouse,
On turning her up in her Nest with the Plough,
November 1785

Wee, sleekit, cowrin, tim'rous beastie,
O, what a panic's in thy breastie!
Thou need na start awa sae hasty,
    Wi' bickering brattle!
I wad be laith to rin an' chase thee,   5
    Wi' murdering pattle!

I'm truly sorry man's dominion
Has broken Nature's social union,
An' justifies that ill opinion
    Which makes thee startle   10
At me, thy poor, earth-born companion
    An' fellow mortal!

I doubt na, whyles, but thou may thieve;
What then? poor beastie, thou maun live!
A daimen icker in a thrave   15
    'S a sma' request;
I'll get a blessin wi' the lave,
    An' never miss't!

Thy wee-bit housie, too, in ruin!
Its silly wa's the win's are strewin!   20
An' naething, now, to big a new ane,
    O' foggage green!
An' bleak December's win's ensuin,
    Baith snell an' keen!

29 *coulter:*   plough blade

31 *stibble:*   stubble

34 *But house or hald:*   without house or holding

35 *thole:*   endure

36 *cranreuch:*   hoar-frost

37 *thy lane:*   alone

40 *Gang aft agley:*   go often off the straight

✦ *Activities*

1 *Wee* is the first word of the poem. Pick out all the other words which convey the small scale of the mouse's life. Explain how this emphasis on the fragility of the mouse's life contributes to the theme of the poem.

2 What does Burns think he has in common with the mouse and what makes him different?

3 You have met a sheep farmer whose lambs are occasionally taken by a rare species of eagle (or a fisherman whose catch is reduced by seals; or a builder who plans to build in a wood inhabited by badgers). Improvise a discussion in pairs, with one of you putting forward Burns's philosophy about respect for wild animals, and the other representing the point of view of the person whose interests clash with that. First make plans and notes.

Thou saw the fields laid bare an' waste,   25
An' weary winter comin fast,
An' cozie here, beneath the blast,
        Thou thought to dwell,
Till crash! the cruel coulter past
        Out thro' thy cell.   30

That wee bit heap o' leaves an' stibble,
Has cost thee monie a weary nibble!
Now thou's turned out, for a' thy trouble,
        But house or hald,
To thole the winter's sleety dribble,   35
        An' cranreuch cauld!

But Mousie, thou art no thy lane,
In proving foresight may be vain:
The best-laid schemes o' mice an' men
        Gang aft agley,   40
An' lea'e us nought but grief an' pain,
        For promis'd joy!

Still thou art blest, compared wi' me!
The present only toucheth thee:
But och! I backward cast my e'e,   45
        On prospects drear!
An' forward, tho' I canna see,
        I guess an' fear!

Notes on 'Love and Liberty – a cantata' or 'The Jolly Beggars'

Background

This is the last song of nine in a 'cantata' (Burns's word) which shows a group of lusty beggars making merry in a low-class inn. It probably arose from a visit which Burns paid to Poosie Nancie's inn-cum-brothel in Mauchline as a young tearaway farmer. Amongst the ragged company in the cantata are a disabled old soldier, a regimental prostitute, a professional clown, a stunted fiddler, a tinker and a ballad singer. This is the final song of the piece, sung by the ballad singer.

Hearty beggars were traditionally regarded as the embodiment of carefree liberty, and there was a long line of songs going back to the Middle Ages (*chansons de gueux*) celebrating their way of life. The tune is English and of more recent origin.

Verse form

Four-beat lines rhyming abab.

---

16 *doxies:*   women; a word from the jargon of beggars in English and Scots

17 *train-attended:*   followed by servants

Love and Liberty – a cantata (or *The Jolly Beggars*)
Final Air

TUNE: *Jolly Mortals, Fill Your Glasses*

See the smoking bowl before us!
    Mark our jovial, ragged ring!
Round and round take up the chorus,
    And in raptures let us sing:

Chorus
    A fig for those by law protected!   5
      Liberty's a glorious feast,
    Courts for cowards were erected,
      Churches built to please the priest!

What is title, what is treasure,
    What is reputation's care?   10
If we lead a life of pleasure,
    'Tis no matter how or where!

With the ready trick and fable
    Round we wander all the day;
And at night in barn or stable   15
    Hug our doxies on the hay.

Does the train-attended carriage
    Thro' the country lighter rove?
Does the sober bed of marriage
    Witness brighter scenes of love?   20

21 & 23 *variorum* and *decorum:* The rhyme scheme gives prominence to these two noticeably Latinate words. Why do you think this is?
    25 *budgets:* leather pouches
            wallets: beggars' bags
    27 *callets:* wenches; an old word used in English and Scots

---

✦ *Activities*

1 Work out the singer's ideas about:
- the particular pleasures of a beggar's life;
- the values of a settled society which the beggars reject.

2 The language of this poem is almost entirely English. Is this out of dramatic character? Does the choice of language lend weight to the ideas, as is the case in 'Scots, wha hae' (p. 117) and 'Such a parcel of rogues' (p. 115)? Consider also the note to lines 21 and 23.

3 Put together a choral verse speaking of these rousing words. Select single voices for aspects of the poem and vary the number of people who speak to provide variety of volume.

4 The cotter of 'The Cotter's Saturday Night' (p. 41) discovers an old beggar from this group lying abandoned and dying in his outhouse. Script their conversation.

Or:

An able-bodied beggar from this gang is about to be hanged for stealing. He is allowed to make a last speech from the scaffold to the crowd of solid citizens, churchgoers, poor farm workers and half-starved town riff-raff. Write it and deliver it.

Life is all a variorum,
    We regard not how it goes;
Let them prate about decorum,
    Who have character to lose.

Here's to budgets, bags, and wallets!   25
    Here's to all the wandering train!
Here's our ragged brats and callets!
    One and all, cry out, Amen!

Chorus
    A fig for those by law protected!
        Liberty's a glorious feast,   30
    Courts for cowards were erected,
        Churches built to please the priest!

Notes on 'To William Simpson, Ochiltree'

Background
William Simpson was a schoolmaster in Ochiltree, Ayrshire. He had written a verse letter to Burns, praising his poetry, which was circulating in manuscript. The verse letter was an established form in Roman, Scots and English literature.

Verse form
Standard Habbie (see page 180).

---

2 *brawlie:*   handsomely

3 *maun:*   must

4 *unco:*   unusually

7 *I'se:*   I shall

8 *sud:*   should
laith: loath

9 *sidelins sklented:*   sideways squinted

10 *Musie:*   Burns's Muse, or spirit of poetic inspiration, becomes self-mocking and homely with the addition of the Scots diminutive '-ie'.

11 *phraisin:*   praising

13 *wad be in a creel:*   would be in a basket

14 *speel:*   climb

15 The Scots poet Allan Ramsay (1685–1758) had carried on a correspondence in rhyme with the minor poet William Hamilton of Gilbertfield (c1665–1751).

16 *braes:*   Perhaps the slopes of Mount Parnassus are intended, the mountain where the Muses of Greek legend dwelt.

17–24 Robert Fergusson (1750–74) had had to work as a humble clerk in an Edinburgh law firm even though he was the most talented Scots poet of his time.

17 *writer-chiel:*   lawyer fellow

21 *whunstane:*   whinstone

23 *tythe:*   tenth   *cartes:*   cards

24 *wad stow'd:*   would have stored

To William Simpson, Ochiltree

May — 1785.

I gat your letter, winsome Willie;
Wi' gratefu' heart I thank you brawlie;
Tho' I maun say't, I wad be silly
      And unco vain,
Should I believe, my coaxin billie,   5
      Your flatterin strain.

But I'se believe ye kindly meant it:
I sud be laith to think ye hinted
Ironic satire, sidelins sklented,
      On my poor Musie;   10
Tho' in sic phraisin terms ye've penn'd it,
      I scarce excuse ye.

My senses wad be in a creel,
Should I but dare a hope to speel,
Wi' Allan, or wi' Gilbertfield,   15
      The braes o' fame;
Or Fergusson, the writer-chiel,
      A deathless name.

(O Fergusson! thy glorious parts
Ill suited law's dry, musty arts!   20
My curse upon your whunstane hearts,
      Ye E'nbrugh gentry!
The tythe o' what ye waste at cartes
      Wad stow'd his pantry!)

26 *screed:* wrench

27 *whiles:* sometimes

29 *rustic reed:* This is the conventional imagery of 18th-century poetry, derived from ancient classical sources. It sees the poet as a shepherd playing upon Pan pipes – hence the *reed*. This fitted in with Burns's country background. *Bardies* (line 32) and *lays* (line 34) refer to another classical idea of the poet as chanting his verses. *Chanters* (line 33) is a witty variation peculiarly suited to Scottish poets. The chanter is the finger pipe of the bagpipes.

31 *Coila:* Burns's idea of a protective goddess or personification of Kyle, his district of Ayrshire
fidge fu' fain: squirm with delight

32 *bardies:* poets like William Simpson and Burns

33 *Chiels:* fellows
hain: save

38 *in measur'd style:* in verse written with a beat

40–42 *New Holland* was the then unexplored territory now known as Western Australia. The coastline had been discovered by the Dutch in the early 1600s.
Magellan refers to the Strait of Magellan at the southern tip of South America.

44 *aboon:* above
Forth, Tay, Yarrow, Tweed: rivers of Scotland

46 *Owre:* over

47 *Irwin*, *Lugar*, *Ayr* and *Doon* are rivers of Burns's native Ayrshire.

49 *Illissus*, *Tiber*, *Thames* and *Seine* are respectively rivers of Athens, Rome, London and Paris. These represent the great literature of ancient Greece and Rome, of England and of France.

51–52 The image here is of Burns and Simpson standing side by side (foot next to foot) and setting their helmets straight before taking on the poets of the world in poetic battle.

Yet when a tale comes i' my head,   25
Or lasses gie my heart a screed—
As whiles they're like to be my dead,
            (O sad disease!)
I kittle up my rustic reed;
                It gies me ease.   30

Auld Coila, now, may fidge fu' fain,
She's gotten bardies o' her ain;
Chiels wha their chanters winna hain,
                But tune their lays,
Till echoes a' resound again   35
                Her weel-sung praise.

Nae Poet thought her worth his while,
To set her name in measur'd style;
She lay like some unkend-of isle
                Beside New Holland,   40
Or whare wild-meeting oceans boil
                Besouth Magellan.

Ramsay an' famous Fergusson
Gied Forth an' Tay a lift aboon;
Yarrow an' Tweed, to monie a tune,   45
                Owre Scotland rings,
While Irwin, Lugar, Ayr, an' Doon,
                Naebody sings.

Th' Illissus, Tiber, Thames an' Seine,
Glide sweet in monie a tunefu' line: 50
But, Willie, set your fit to mine,
                An' cock your crest!
We'll gar our streams and burnies shine
                Up wi' the best.

55 *fells:* hills

55–90 In this passage Burns reveals his love of Nature. Note the characteristic language forms of this passage: the plurals and the frequent use of *the*.
What effect do these have on the character of the description?

58–64 *Wallace:* Sir William Wallace (c 1270–1305), the patriot who led the Scots against the oppressive occupation by King Edward I of England before Bruce declared himself King of Scots

59 *bure the gree:* bore off the prize

60 *Suthron billies:* southern fellows

65 *red-wat-shod:* shoes wet with red

66 *dy'd:* died

67 *haughs:* water-meadows

69 *jinkin:* darting
whids: races

71 *cushat:* wood pigeon

We'll sing auld Coila's plains an' fells,   55
Her moors red-brown wi' heather bells,
Her banks an' braes, her dens an' dells,
                Whare glorious Wallace
Aft bure the gree, as story tells,
                Frae Suthron billies.   60

At Wallace' name, what Scottish blood
But boils up in a spring-tide flood?
Oft have our fearless fathers strode
                By Wallace' side,
Still pressing onward, red-wat-shod,   65
                Or glorious dy'd!

O, sweet are Coila's haughs an' woods,
When lintwhites chant amang the buds,
And jinkin hares, in amorous whids,
                Their loves enjoy;   70
While thro' the braes the cushat croods
                With wailfu' cry!

Ev'n winter bleak has charms to me,
When winds rave thro' the naked tree;
Or frosts on hills of Ochiltree   75
                Are hoary gray;
Or blinding drifts wild-furious flee,
                Dark'ning the day!

O Nature! a' thy shews an' forms
To feeling, pensive hearts hae charms!   80
Whether the summer kindly warms,
                Wi' life an' light;
Or winter howls, in gusty storms,
                The lang, dark night!

85 *fand:* found

88 *An' no think lang:* and not think that the time was too long

91 *warly:* worldly

92 *Hog-shouther:* push
jundie: jostle

93 *descrive:* describe

96 *Bum:* hum

98 *owre lang unkend to ither:* too long unknown to each other

101 *May Envy wallop in a tether:* jerk in a hangman's noose; an example of personification of an abstraction. Compare with 'Tam o' Shanter' lines 53–54 and 'The Cotter's Saturday Night' line 76. Which of these examples has a different effect and why?

104 *braxies:* sheep that have died of a disease that was considered to make them particularly tasty

---

✦ *Activities*

1 Photocopy this poem. Using different coloured markers, highlight the various subject matters that you can find. Discuss the links between them. Devise different signs and arrows to show loose links and close ones. Decide what unifying theme there is, if any.

2 This poem was actually sent as a letter. What characteristics of a personal letter does it show?

3 Examine this poem for exclusively Scots words, words common to both Scots and English but given in their Scots form, and Standard English words. You could set this out in the form of a Venn Diagram: two large circles which overlap with each other, giving common ground in the middle. Write each word into the appropriate space.

Can you detect any connection between choice of language, subject matter and mood?

The Muse, nae poet ever fand her,   85
Till by himsel he learn'd to wander,
Adown some trottin burn's meander,
            An' no think lang:
O, sweet to stray an' pensive ponder
            A heart-felt sang!   90

The warly race may drudge an' drive,
Hog-shouther, jundie, stretch, an' strive;
Let me fair Nature's face descrive,
            And I, wi' pleasure,
Shall let the busy, grumbling hive   95
            Bum owre their treasure.

Fareweel, my rhyme-composing brither!
We've been owre lang unkend to ither:
Now let us lay our heads thegither,
            In love fraternal: 100
May Envy wallop in a tether,
            Black fiend, infernal!

While Highlandmen hate tolls an' taxes;
While moorlan' herds like guid, fat braxies;
While Terra Firma, on her axis,   105
            Diurnal turns;
Count on a friend, in faith an' practice,
            In Robert Burns.

* * * * * *

[*At this point Burns adds a Postscript which is completely self-contained and unrelated to the main body of the letter. It is a satirical description of the conflicting theological factions of the Church in Scotland.*]

Notes on 'The Cotter's Saturday Night'

Background

A cotter was a hired labourer. Burns's brother, Gilbert, wrote that the father in this poem was directly modelled on their own father, although he was a tenant farmer, a social position superior to a cotter. The personal emotion in the poem derives from this connection. In this poem Burns depicts the life of a rural family, partly idealising memories of his own childhood and partly reflecting the fashionable belief in the virtues of the simple life (see page 166).

Verse form

Spenserian stanza (see page 181).

The epigraph at the head of the poem is a verse from 'Elegy Written in a Country Church-yard' (published 1751) by Thomas Gray, which develops the theme of the innate worth of the unknown members of the peasantry. (See extract on page 140.)

---

4 & 9 *meed, ween:* archaic words showing the influence of Spenser (see page 181)
meed: reward

5 See note to line 29 ('To William Simpson, Ochiltree'), page 34.

6 *train:* way of life
life's sequester'd scene: Compare with Gray's 'Elegy': *cool sequester'd vale of life*. (See page 141.)

8 *Aiken:* Robert Aiken was a lawyer in Ayr. He encouraged Burns to value his own poetry and to publish it. He was the same Aiken who is mentioned in 'Holy Willie's Prayer' (page 9).

9 *ween:* think

10 *sugh:* blast

10–18 Compare with Gray's 'Elegy' (page 140): *The ploughman homeward plods his weary way*, etc.

The Cotter's Saturday Night
Inscribed to R. Aiken, Esq.

Let not Ambition mock their useful toil,
Their homely joys, and destiny obscure;
Nor Grandeur hear, with a disdainful smile,
The short and simple annals of the Poor.

Gray.

I

My lov'd, my honor'd, much respected friend!
   No mercenary bard his homage pays;
With honest pride, I scorn each selfish end,
   My dearest meed, a friend's esteem and praise:
   To you I sing, in simple Scottish lays,   5
The lowly train in life's sequester'd scene;
   The native feelings strong, the guileless ways;
What Aiken in a cottage would have been;
Ah! tho' his worth unknown, far happier there, I ween!

II

November chill blaws loud wi' angry sugh;   10
   The short'ning winter-day is near a close;
The miry beasts retreating frae the pleugh;
   The black'ning trains o' craws to their repose:
   The toil-worn Cotter frae his labor goes—
This night his weekly moil is at an end,   15
   Collects his spades, his mattocks, and his hoes,
Hoping the morn in ease and rest to spend,
And weary, o'er the moor, his course does hameward bend.

21 *stacher:* totter
22 *flichterin':* fluttering
23 *ingle:* fire
26 *kiaugh:* anxiety; one of Burns's words from his local dialect of Kyle
28 *Belyve:* by and by
29 *service:* Although some features of Burns's description of this family derive from memories of his own childhood, his own father and he himself ranked as farmers and not as cotters. Robert was never sent out to work for neighbours.
30 *ca':* drive
   tentie: attentively
31 *cannie:* careful
   town: farmstead
35 *sair-won penny-fee:* hard-won wages
38 *spiers:* asks
40 *uncos:* news
41 *partial:* loving
42 *Anticipation forward points the view:* a typical 18th-century English poetic line – a personification followed by an abstract general expression
44 *Gars auld claes:* makes old clothes
45 *admonition:* the moral warnings which follow in Stanza VI

III

At length his lonely cot appears in view,
    Beneath the shelter of an agèd tree;   20
Th' expectant wee-things, toddlin, stacher through
    To meet their dad, wi' flichterin' noise an' glee.
    His wee bit ingle, blinkin bonilie,
His clean hearth-stane, his thrifty wifie's smile,
    The lisping infant, prattling on his knee,   25
Does a' his weary kiaugh and care beguile,
And makes him quite forget his labor and his toil.

IV

Belyve, the elder bairns come drapping in,
    At service out, amang the farmers roun';
Some ca' the pleugh, some herd, some tentie rin   30
    A cannie errand to a neebor town:
    Their eldest hope, their Jenny, woman grown,
In youthfu' bloom, Love sparkling in her e'e,
    Comes hame; perhaps to shew a braw new gown,
Or deposite her sair-won penny-fee,   35
To help her parents dear, if they in hardship be.

V

With joy unfeign'd, brothers and sisters meet,
    And each for other's weelfare kindly spiers:
The social hours, swift-wing'd, unnotic'd fleet;
    Each tells the uncos that he sees or hears.   40
    The parents, partial, eye their hopeful years;
Anticipation forward points the view.
    The mother, wi' her needle and her sheers,
Gars auld claes look amaist as weel's the new;
The father mixes a' wi' admonition due.   45

48 *eydent:*   diligent
49 *jauk:*   waste time
51 *duty:*   the Christian's obligation to private prayer
52 *gang:*   go
54 *sought the Lord:*   prayed to God
62 *hafflins:*   half

VI

Their master's and their mistress's command,
    The younkers a' are warnèd to obey;
And mind their labors wi' an eydent hand,
    And ne'er, tho' out o' sight, to jauk or play:
    'And O! be sure to fear the Lord alway,   50
And mind your duty, duly, morn and night;
    Lest in temptation's path ye gang astray,
Implore His counsel and assisting might:
They never sought in vain that sought the Lord aright.'

VII

But hark! a rap comes gently to the door;   55
    Jenny, wha kens the meaning o' the same,
Tells how a neebor lad cam o'er the moor,
    To do some errands, and convoy her hame.
    The wily mother sees the conscious flame
Sparkle in Jenny's e'e, and flush her cheek;   60
    With heart-struck anxious care, enquires his name,
While Jenny hafflins is afraid to speak;
Weel pleas'd the mother hears, it's nae wild, worthless rake.

64 *ben:* into the house
67 *cracks:* chats
    kye: cows
69 *blate and laithfu':* shy and bashful
72 *lave:* rest
73–90 Stanzas IX and X adopt a different style from the passages immediately before and after them. To examine this style you will need a dictionary of literary critical terms or the biggest dictionary of English available. Look up definitions of the following terms and locate examples from these stanzas: exclamation (*O happy love!*); personification (*sage Experience*); rhetorical question (*Are Honour, Virtue, Conscience, all exil'd?*); archaism (*Ruth*); circumlocution (*this weary, mortal round*). Try to find other examples in these stanzas and in stanzas XVII and XIX to XXI. You might also find examples of apostrophe and metonymy. What impression does this style make on you? See the Resource Notes on Poetic diction, page 171.
76 *Experience:* a personification – an allegorical figure who is represented as speaking to the poet. This is another expression typical of 18th-century English high poetic style.
78 *cordial:* refreshing drink
    this melancholy vale: earthly life as contrasted with the joys of Heaven

VIII

With kindly welcome, Jenny brings him ben;
   A strappin' youth, he takes the mother's eye;   65
Blythe Jenny sees the visit's no ill taen;
   The father cracks of horses, pleughs, and kye.
   The youngster's artless heart o'erflows wi' joy,
But blate and laithfu', scarce can weel behave;
   The mother, wi' a woman's wiles, can spy   70
What makes the youth sae bashfu' and sae grave;
Weel-pleas'd to think her bairn's respected like the lave.

IX

O happy love! where love like this is found:
   O heart-felt raptures! bliss beyond compare!
I've pacèd much this weary, mortal round,   75
   And sage Experience bids me this declare:—
   'If Heaven a draught of heavenly pleasure spare,
One cordial in this melancholy vale,
   'Tis when a youthful, loving, modest pair,
In other's arms, breathe out the tender tale   80
Beneath the milk-white thorn that scents the ev'ning gale.'

86 *perjur'd:*   making false promises of marriage

88 *Ruth:*   tenderness

83–90 The gulf between Burns's actual behaviour towards young women and the opinions he expresses here shows how completely he has assumed a persona, a personality other than his own, in this poem, with its exclamatory moralisings in imitation of Gray (see page 140).

92 *healsome parritch:*   wholesome porridge

93 *soupe:*   drink

   hawkie: cow

94 *the hallan:*   partition. The family live in a typical peasant homestead like Burns's own birthplace at Alloway, with the living quarters continuous with the byre.

   cood: cud

96 *To grace the lad, her weel-hain'd kebbuck, fell:*   to do honour to the lad, her well-saved cheese, strong

99 *a towmond auld, sin' lint was i' the bell:*   a twelvemonth old since flax was in bloom

100–162 See Religion and Superstition in the Resource Notes on pages 164–165, and also the extract from *A History of the Scottish People 1560–1830* on page 167.

101 *ingle:*   fireplace

103 *ha'-Bible:*   one of Burns's expressions from his local dialect of Kyle; a large family Bible for communal readings

105 *lyart haffets:*   grey side locks

106 *Those strains:*   For better understanding, think of 'from' before 'those'.

   The 'strains' are the strains of music of the Psalms of David in the Old Testament of the Bible, which were sung in the Temple of the Jews on Mount Zion in Jerusalem.

107 *wales:*   chooses

X

Is there, in human form, that bears a heart,
    A wretch! a villain! lost to love and truth!
That can, with studied, sly, ensnaring art,
    Betray sweet Jenny's unsuspecting youth?   85
    Curse on his perjur'd arts! dissembling, smooth!
Are Honor, Virtue, Conscience, all exil'd?
    Is there no Pity, no relenting Ruth,
Points to the parents fondling o'er their child?
Then paints the ruin'd maid, and their distraction wild!   90

XI

But now the supper crowns their simple board,
    The healsome parritch, chief o' Scotia's food;
The soupe their only hawkie does afford,
    That 'yont the hallan snugly chows her cood;
    The dame brings forth, in complimental mood,   95
To grace the lad, her weel-hain'd kebbuck, fell;
    And aft he's prest, and aft he ca's it guid;
The frugal wifie, garrulous, will tell,
How 'twas a towmond auld, sin' lint was i' the bell.

XII

The chearfu' supper done, wi' serious face,   100
    They, round the ingle, form a circle wide;
The sire turns o'er, wi' patriachal grace,
    The big ha'-Bible, ance his father's pride.
    His bonnet rev'rently is laid aside,
His lyart haffets wearing thin and bare;   105
    Those strains that once did sweet in Zion glide,
He wales a portion with judicious care,
And 'Let us worship God!' he says, with solemn air.

111–113 *Dundee*, *Martyrs*, *Elgin:*   tunes in the old Scottish Psalm Book, still occasionally sung

113 *beets:*   feeds. Family worship is being compared here to the offering of a sacrifice on an altar, the flames rising to heaven.

115 *Italian trills:*   the fashionable opera music of the time

118 *the sacred page:*   the Holy Bible

119–120 *Abram, Moses:*   early leaders of the people of Israel.

121 *Amalek:*   the Amalekites, inhabitants of Palestine in conflict with the invading Israelites

122 *the royal Bard:*   King David, reputed author of the Psalms in the Bible, who was punished for his sins by God

125/126 *Isaiah:*   the prophet who supposedly wrote the book of that name in the Old Testament of the Bible
holy Seers: prophets who wrote books of the Old Testament
lyre: In accordance with standard 18th-century convention, the prophets are represented as poets who chanted their words to the accompaniment of a lyre.

127 *the Christian volume:*   the New Testament

128 *guiltless blood:*   Christians believe Jesus was without sin but his blood was shed in the crucifixion to save guilty sinners.

129 *in Heaven the second name:*   Jesus is the second person of the three aspects of the Christian God, the Trinity.

130 *Had not on earth whereon to lay His head:*   Jesus is represented in the Gospels as a wandering preacher.

131 *sped:*   prospered. The father was reading from The Acts of the Apostles.

132 *precepts sage:*   the epistles to the early Christian churches

133 *lone in Patmos:*   St John the Divine, who wrote the Book of Revelation, a vision of the end of the world

135 *great Bab'lon's doom:*   In the Book of Revelation 17, verse 5, Babylon is the code name given to the Roman Empire, which was persecuting Christians.

XIII

They chant their artless notes in simple guise,
    They tune their hearts, by far the noblest aim;   110
Perhaps *Dundee's* wild-warbling measures rise,
    Or plaintive *Martyrs*, worthy of the name;
    Or noble *Elgin* beets the heaven-ward flame,
The sweetest far of Scotia's holy lays:
    Compar'd with these, Italian trills are tame;   115
The tickl'd ears no heart-felt raptures raise;
Nae unison hae they, with our Creator's praise.

XIV

The priest-like father reads the sacred page,
    How Abram was the friend of God on high;
Or, Moses bade eternal warfare wage   120
    With Amalek's ungracious progeny;
    Or, how the royal Bard did groaning lie
Beneath the stroke of Heaven's avenging ire;
    Or Job's pathetic plaint, and wailing cry;
Or rapt Isaiah's wild, seraphic fire;   125
Or other holy Seers that tune the sacred lyre.

XV

Perhaps the Christian volume is the theme:
    How guiltless blood for guilty man was shed;
How He, who bore in Heaven the second name,
    Had not on earth whereon to lay His head;   130
    How His first followers and servants sped;
The precepts sage they wrote to many a land:
    How he, who lone in Patmos, banishèd,
Saw in the sun a mighty angel stand,
And heard great Bab'lon's doom pronounc'd by Heaven's   135
    command.

138 *'springs exulting on triumphant wing':* a misquotation from 'Windsor Forest' (1713) by Alexander Pope (1688–1744), the dominant figure in 18th-century English poetry

139 *future days:* after death

140 *uncreated rays:* the divine light of Heaven, which has existed from all eternity, as has God Himself

144 In the eternity of Heaven, time never progresses.

145 *Religion:* formal church services, perhaps especially the more elaborate episcopalian kind

149 *The Power:* God or the Holy Spirit, which is the presence of God

150 *sacerdotal stole:* priestly robe

153 *His Book of Life:* the book mentioned in Revelation 20, verse 15, in which the names of the saved souls are written: *And whosoever was not found written in the book of life was cast into the lake of fire.*

158 *raven's:* See St Luke 12, verse 24: *Consider the ravens: for they neither sow nor reap; which neither have storehouse nor barn; and God feedeth them: how much more are ye better than the fowls?*

159 *lily:* See St Matthew 6, verse 28: *Consider the lilies of the field, how they grow; they toil not, neither do they spin: And yet I say unto you, That Solomon in all his glory was not arrayed like one of these.*

ROBERT BURNS

XVI

Then kneeling down to Heaven's Eternal King,
    The saint, the father, and the husband prays:
Hope 'springs exulting on triumphant wing',
    That thus they all shall meet in future days,
    There, ever bask in uncreated rays,   140
No more to sigh or shed the bitter tear,
    Together hymning their Creator's praise,
In such society, yet still more dear;
While circling Time moves round in an eternal sphere.

XVII

Compar'd with this, how poor Religion's pride,   145
    In all the pomp of method, and of art;
When men display to congregations wide
    Devotion's ev'ry grace, except the heart!
    The Power, incens'd, the pageant will desert,
The pompous strain, the sacerdotal stole: 150
    But haply, in some cottage far apart,
May hear, well-pleas'd, the language of the soul,
And in His Book of Life the inmates poor enroll.

XVIII

Then homeward all take off their sev'ral way;
    The youngling cottagers retire to rest: 155
The parent-pair their secret homage pay,
    And proffer up to Heaven the warm request,
    That He who stills the raven's clam'rous nest,
And decks the lily fair in flow'ry pride,
    Would, in the way His wisdom sees the best,   160
For them and for their little ones provide;
But, chiefly, in their hearts with Grace Divine preside.

53

165 *breath:* Ordinary men are made into nobles by the mere word of the king. Compare this with line 25 from 'For a' that and a' that' (page 123): *A prince can mak' a belted knight.*

166 *'An honest man's the noblest work of God':* This is a quotation from *An Essay on Man* by Alexander Pope (1688–1744).

167 *certes:* certainly; another archaic form designed to lend dignity to the style

176 *prevent:* protect

XIX

From scenes like these, old Scotia's grandeur springs,
    That makes her lov'd at home, rever'd abroad:
Princes and lords are but the breath of kings,   165
    'An honest man's the noblest work of God';
    And certes, in fair Virtue's heavenly road,
The Cottage leaves the Palace far behind;
    What is a lordling's pomp? a cumbrous load,
Disguising oft the wretch of human kind,   170
Studied in arts of Hell, in wickedness refin'd!

XX

O Scotia! my dear, my native soil!
    For whom my warmest wish to Heaven is sent!
Long may thy hardy sons of rustic toil
    Be blest with health, and peace, and sweet content!   175
    And O! may Heaven their simple lives prevent
From Luxury's contagion, weak and vile!
    Then, howe'er crowns and coronets be rent,
A virtuous populace may rise the while,
And stand a wall of fire around their much-lov'd Isle.   180

182–184 *Wallace:* See note on page 36. He was executed as a traitor by King Edward I of England in 1305, although he had never sworn allegiance to the English king.

✦ *Activities*

1 This poem starts as an address, contains a narrative with descriptions and ends as a prayer. Identify any other elements you can find in your reading and label each part of the poem according to its genre and also its particular subject matter.

2 There are at least two distinct styles of writing in this poem. Select some passages which demonstrate this most clearly and discuss how the use of these different styles affects your attitude to Burns's subject matter.

3 There is a 'story', a succession of events, which runs through this poem. Write the dialogue for a radio drama which tells the 'tale'. Use your own local dialect or Burns's. You could tape record the result. (You might then discuss how each event is chosen by Burns to show an aspect of ideal living.)

4 In pairs, let one person take on the role of Burns, the man as you know him from his actual life and his poems. Let the other be a reporter from the *Edinburgh Evening News*. The reporter should question Burns about the relationships between his attitudes as expressed in this poem and as demonstrated in his life. Reverse the roles. Each person should then write a feature article for the newspaper based on the interview.

XXI

O Thou! who pour'd the patriotic tide,
    That stream'd thro' Wallace's undaunted heart,
Who dar'd to, nobly, stem tyrannic pride,
    Or nobly die, the second glorious part:
    (The patriot's God, peculiarly Thou art,   185
His friend, inspirer, guardian, and reward!)
    O never, never Scotia's realm desert;
But still the patriot, and the patriot-bard
In bright succession raise, her ornament and guard!

Notes on 'The Twa Dogs'

Verse form
Octosyllabic couplets – the metre of 'Tam o' Shanter' four years later.

---

 2 *Coil or Kyle:* a district of Ayrshire. King Coil was one of the legendary kings of the Kingdom of Strathclyde in the Dark Ages.
 5 *thrang:* busy
 11 *whalpit:* whelped
 12 *Where sailors gang to fish for cod:* Caesar is a Newfoundland breed of dog.
 13 *braw:* fine
 15 *degree:* rank
 16 *fient:* devil, fiend
 17 *wad:* would
 18 *messin:* cur; one of Burns's words from the local dialect of Kyle
 20 *tawted tyke:* shaggy mongrel
 duddie: tattered
 21 *wad stan't:* would have stood
 22 *stroan't:* pissed
 23 *tither:* other. The 'ploughman' is Burns himself, and line 24 is his own self portrait.
 24 *billie:* fellow
 26 *Luath:* the name of Burns's own beloved collie dog
 27 *Highland sang:* Burns had read James Macpherson's 'translation' (1762) of poems he claimed were ancient Gaelic epics written by a mythical poet, Ossian. Burns's pose as the half-informed 'ploughman' should not be taken at face value. He was a tenant farmer, entitled to be addressed by the name of his farm, Mossgiel.
 28 *lang syne:* long ago

The Twa Dogs
(A Tale)

'Twas in that place o' Scotland's isle
That bears the name of auld King Coil,
Upon a bonie day in June,
When wearing thro' the afternoon,
Twa dogs, that were na thrang at hame,   5
Forgathered ance upon a time.

   The first I'll name, they ca'd him Caesar,
Was keepit for 'his Honor's' pleasure:
His hair, his size, his mouth, his lugs,
Shew'd he was nane o' Scotland's dogs;   10
But whalpit some place far abroad,
Whare sailors gang to fish for cod.

   His lockèd, letter'd, braw brass collar
Shew'd him the gentleman an' scholar;
But tho' he was o' high degree,   15
The fient a pride, nae pride had he;
But wad hae spent an hour caressin,
Ev'n wi' a tinkler-gipsy's messin;
At kirk or market, mill or smiddie,
Nae tawted tyke, tho' e'er sae duddie,   20
But he wad stan't, as glad to see him,
An' stroan't on stanes an' hillocks wi' him.

   The tither was a ploughman's collie,
A rhyming, ranting, raving billie,
Wha for his friend an' comrade had him,   25
And in his freaks had Luath ca'd him,
After some dog in Highland sang,
Was made lang syne—Lord knows how lang.

29 *gash:* clever
30 *lap:* leaped
    sheugh: ditch
    dyke: wall
31 *sonsie:* good-natured
    baws'nt: striped; typically a farmer's word
32 *Ay:* always
    gat: got
    ilka: each
33 *towsie:* shaggy
35 *gawsie:* fine
36 *hurdies:* backside
37 *fain o' ither:* fond of each other
38 *unco pack an' thick thegither:* very intimate together
39 *whyles:* sometimes
    snowkit: poked about
40 *moudieworts:* moles
    howkit: dug up
43 *monie:* many
    farce: frolic
50 *ava:* at all
51 *rackèd:* extortionate
52 *kain:* payment in the form of goods
    stents: taxes
57 *steeks:* stitches
58 *Geordie:* guinea coin – so called because of the head
    of King George on them

He was a gash an' faithfu' tyke,
As ever lap a sheugh or dyke. 30
His honest, sonsie, baws'nt face
Ay gat him friends in ilka place;
His breast was white, his towsie back
Weel clad wi' coat o' glossy black;
His gawsie tail, wi' upward curl, 35
Hung owre his hurdies wi' a swirl.

Nae doubt but they were fain o' ither,
And unco pack an' thick thegither;
Wi' social nose whyles snuff'd an' snowkit;
Whyles mice an' moudieworts they howkit; 40
Whyles scour'd awa' in lang excursion,
An' worry'd ither in diversion;
Till tir'd at last wi' monie a farce,
They sat them down upon their arse,
An' there began a lang digression 45
About the 'lords o' the creation'.

CAESAR

I've aften wonder'd, honest Luath,
What sort o' life poor dogs like you have;
An' when the gentry's life I saw,
What way poor bodies liv'd ava. 50

Our laird gets in his rackèd rents,
His coals, his kain, an' a' his stents;
He rises when he likes himsel;
His flunkies answer at the bell;
He ca's his coach; he ca's his horse; 55
He draws a bonie silken purse,
As lang's my tail, whare, thro' the steeks,
The yellow letter'd Geordie keeks.

59 *e'en:*   evening
61 *stechin:*   stuffing themselves
62 *pechan:*   stomach
65 *whipper-in:*   the servant employed to prevent dogs
  straying from the pack of hounds during a hunt
  blastit wonner: stunted wonder
69 *cot-folk:*   cottagers
  painch: stomach
71 *whyles:*   sometimes
  fash't: troubled
72 *cotter:*   a paid labourer. Burns, his father and his
  brother were tenant farmers and thus in the middle of
  the three social classes in the Scottish countryside:
  laird, tenant and cotter (see line 178).
  howkin: digging
  sheugh: ditch
73 *biggin:*   building
74 *baring:*   uncovering
  sic: such
76 *smytrie:*   collection
  duddie: ragged
77 *han' darg:*   work
78 *thack:*   thatch
  rape: rope
79 *sair:*   sore
80 *want:*   lack
81 *maist:*   almost
82 *maun starve:*   must die
83 *kend:*   knew
85 *buirdly chiels:*   stalwart fellows
  hizzies: girls

Frae morn to e'en it's nought but toiling,
At baking, roasting, frying, boiling;   60
An' tho' the gentry first are stechin,
Yet ev'n the ha' folk fill their pechan
Wi' sauce, ragouts, an' sic like trashtrie,
That's little short o' downright wastrie.
Our whipper-in, wee, blastit wonner,   65
Poor, worthless elf, it eats a dinner,
Better than onie tenant-man
His Honor has in a' the lan';
An' what poor cot-folk pit their painch in,
I own it's past my comprehension.   70

LUATH

Trowth, Caesar, whyles they're fash't eneugh:
A cotter howkin in a sheugh,
Wi' dirty stanes biggin a dyke,
Baring a quarry, an' sic like,
Himsel, a wife, he thus sustains,   75
A smytrie o' wee duddie weans,
An' nought but his han' darg to keep
Them right an' tight in thack an' rape.

An' when they meet wi' sair disasters,
Like loss o' health or want o' masters,   80
Ye maist wad think, a wee touch langer,
An' they maun starve o' cauld and hunger:
But how it comes, I never kend yet,
They're maistly wonderfu' contented;
An' buirdly chiels, an' clever hizzies,   85
Are bred in sic a way as this is.

90 *sic cattle:*   such creatures
91 *gang as saucy:* go as insultingly
92 *wad:*   would
     brock: badger
93 *laird's court-day:*   Tenants of a large landowner were
     required to come personally to the 'big house' with the
     money and farm produce ('kain') they owed as rent.
94 *wae:*   sad
96 *thole:*   endure
     The factor was the senior servant employed by the laird
     to look after the business affairs of the laird's land
     holdings.
     snash: abuse
96–100 This description is drawn from Burns's own experience,
     as his father's farm at Mount Oliphant failed financially
     in 1776. In a letter he wrote: 'The farm proved a ruinous
     bargain; and, to clench the curse, we fell into the hands
     of a factor who sat for the picture I have drawn of one in
     my Tale of two dogs.'
98 *poind:*   seize
99 *maun:*   must
103 *'s ane wad:*   as one would
104 *poortith:*   poverty
109 *close:*   constant
110 *blink:*   moment

CAESAR

But then, to see how ye're negleckit,
How huff'd, an' cuff'd, an' disrespeckit!
Lord man, our gentry care as little
For delvers, ditchers, an' sic cattle;   90
They gang as saucy by poor folk,
As I wad by a stinking brock.

I've notic'd, on our laird's court-day,
(An' monie a time my heart's been wae),
Poor tenant bodies, scant o' cash,   95
How they maun thole a factor's snash:
He'll stamp an' threaten, curse an' swear
He'll apprehend them, poind their gear;
While they maun staun', wi' aspect humble,
An' hear it a', an' fear an' tremble!   100

I see how folk live that hae riches;
But surely poor-folk maun be wretches!

LUATH

They're nae sae wretched 's ane wad think:
Tho' constantly on poortith's brink,
They're sae accustom'd wi' the sight,   105
The view o't gies them little fright.

Then chance an' fortune are sae guided,
They're ay in less or mair provided;
An' tho' fatigu'd wi' close employment,
A blink o' rest's a sweet enjoyment.   110

112 *grushie:* thriving

115 *whyles:* sometimes

nappy: ale

116 *unco:* very

119 *patronage:* One of the long-running disputes which led to divisions in the Christian church in Scotland in the 18th century was about who had the right to appoint clergymen to parishes. These matters were taken very seriously by the common people. The more extreme presbyterian view was that the members of the parish church should have the only say, a view which did not suit the Crown or the aristocrats. The opposing view was that the land owner (the 'patron') or the group of leading land owners in the parish (the 'heritors') had the right to 'present' a clergyman to the parish.

122 *ferlie:* marvel

123 *bleak-fac'd:* because it is the beginning of winter

Hallowmass: All Saints' Day – Hallowe'en – 31st October

124 *kirn:* harvest home; a large party and dance to celebrate the safe gathering of the harvest

125 *station:* rank

127 *blinks:* glances

129 *That merry day the year begins:* New Year's Day

131 *nappy:* ale

reeks: smokes

ream: froth

133 *luntin:* smoking

sneeshin mill: snuff box

135 *cantie:* cheery

crackin crouse: gossiping merrily

136 *ranting:* romping

137 *fain:* glad

139 *owre:* too

140 *sic:* such

owre aften: too often

The dearest comfort o' their lives,
Their grushie weans an' faithfu' wives;
The prattling things are just their pride,
That sweetens a' their fire-side.

An' whyles twalpennie worth o' nappy   115
Can mak the bodies unco happy:
They lay aside their private cares,
To mind the Kirk and State affairs;
They'll talk o' patronage an' priests,
Wi' kindling fury i' their breasts,   120
Or tell what new taxation's comin,
An' ferlie at the folk in Lon'on.

As bleak-fac'd Hallowmass returns,
They get the jovial, ranting kirns,
When rural life, of ev'ry station,   125
Unite in common recreation;
Love blinks, Wit slaps, an' social Mirth
Forgets there's Care upo' the earth.

That merry day the year begins,
They bar the door on frosty win's;   130
The nappy reeks wi' mantling ream,
An' sheds a heart-inspiring steam;
The luntin pipe, an' sneeshin mill,
Are handed round wi' right guid will;
The cantie auld folks crackin crouse,   135
The young anes ranting thro' the house—
My heart has been sae fain to see them,
That I for joy hae barkit wi' them.

Still it's owre true that ye hae said,
Sic game is now owre aften play'd;   140
There's monie a creditable stock

142 *fawsont:*   respectable
146 *gentle:*   upper class
147 *aiblins:*   perhaps
    thrang: busy
148 *saul:*   soul
    indentin: pledging
149 *Haith:*   faith
    ken: know
150 *guid:*   good
151 *gaun:*   going
158 *bon ton:*   (French) good taste
160 *entails:*   An entail is a legal document by which a rich man ensures that after his death his money is handed down to future generations exactly according to his wishes. The father's intention was to prevent his son using up the estate or disposing of it according to his own wishes. The spendthrift laird defeats the purpose of his father's will by spending all the money himself.
162 *fecht wi' nowt:*   fight with cattle
165 *drumlie:*   muddy
    German water: The laird stays at a German health resort and drinks the mineral waters as a health cure.
167 *consequential sorrows:*   The laird has contracted syphilis or some other venereal disease as a consequence of intercourse with loose-living foreign women during a carnival.

O' decent, honest, fawsont folk,
Are riven out baith root an' branch,
Some rascal's pridefu' greed to quench,
Wha thinks to knit himsel the faster   145
In favor wi' some gentle master,
Wha, aiblins thrang a parliamentin',
For Britain's guid his saul indentin'—

CAESAR

Haith, lad, ye little ken about it:
For Britain's guid! guid faith! I doubt it.   150
Say rather, gaun as Premiers lead him:
An' saying aye or no's they bid him:
At operas an' plays parading,
Mortgaging, gambling, masquerading:
Or maybe, in a frolic daft,   155
To Hague or Calais taks a waft,
To mak a tour, an' tak a whirl,
To learn *bon ton*, an' see the worl'.

There, at Vienna or Versailles,
He rives his father's auld entails;   160
Or by Madrid he taks the rout,
To thrum guitars an' fecht wi' nowt;
Or down Italian vista startles,
Whore-hunting amang groves o' myrtles:
Then bowses drumlie German water,   165
To mak himsel look fair an' fatter,
An' clear the consequential sorrows,
Love-gifts of Carnival signoras.

For Britain's guid! for her destruction!
Wi' dissipation, feud an' faction.   170

171 *gate:*   way
172 *braw:*   fine
173 *foughten:*   troubled
174 *gear tae gang that gate:*   wealth to go that way
179 *rantin, ramblin billies:*   jolly, roistering fellows
180 *Fient haet o' them:*   Devil a one of them
181 *timmer:*   timber
182 *limmer:*   mistress
187 *steer:*   trouble
188 *vera:*   very
     fear: frighten
189 *whyles:*   sometimes
190 *wad:*   would
193 *sair:*   hard
     banes: bones
194 *grips:*   gripes
     granes: groans

LUATH

Hech man! dear sirs! is that the gate
They waste sae monie a braw estate!
Are we sae foughten an' harass'd
For gear tae gang that gate at last?

O would they stay aback frae courts,   175
An' please themsels wi' countra sports,
It wad for ev'ry ane be better,
The laird, the tenant, an' the cotter!
For thae frank, rantin, ramblin billies,
Fient haet o' them's ill-hearted fellows: 180
Except for breakin o' their timmer,
Or speakin lightly o' their limmer,
Or shootin of a hare or moor-cock,
The ne'er-a-bit they're ill to poor folk.

But will ye tell me, master Caesar: 185
Sure great folk's life's a life o' pleasure?
Nae cauld nor hunger e'er can steer them,
The vera thought o't need na fear them.

CAESAR

Lord, man, were ye but whyles whare I am,
The gentles, ye wad ne'er envy 'em!   190

It's true, they need na starve or sweat,
Thro' winter's cauld, or simmer's heat;
They've nae sair wark to craze their banes,
An' fill auld-age wi' grips an' granes:
But human bodies are sic fools,   195
For a' their colleges an' schools,

198 *enow:*   enough
199 *ay:*   always
   sturt: annoy
203 *wheel:*   spinning wheel
204 *dizzen:*   dozen lengths
   unco: very
205 *warst:*   worst
206 *ev'n down want o' wark:*   downright lack of work
208 *deil-haet:*   devil a thing
213 *sic:*   such
215 *cast out in party-matches:*   fall out in political disputes
216 *sowther:*   solder together
222 *a' run:*   downright
   jads: an abusive word for a woman (a jade, or worn-out horse)
225 *lee-lang:*   live-long
   crabbit leuks: ill-natured looks
226 *the devil's pictur'd beuks:*   playing cards. The church authorities disapproved of card games because of their association with gambling.

That when nae real ills perplex them,
They mak enow themsels to vex them;
An' ay the less they hae to sturt them,
In like proportion, less will hurt them.   200

    A countra fellow at the pleugh,
His acre's till'd, he's right eneugh;
A countra girl at her wheel,
Her dizzen's done, she's unco weel;
But gentlemen, an' ladies warst,   205
Wi' ev'n down want o' wark are curst:
They loiter, lounging, lank an' lazy;
Tho' deil-haet ails them, yet uneasy:
Their days insipid, dull an' tasteless;
Their nights unquiet, lang an' restless.   210

    An' ev'n their sports, their balls an' races,
Their galloping through public places,
There's sic parade, sic pomp an' art,
The joy can scarcely reach the heart.

    The men cast out in party-matches,   215
Then sowther a' in deep debauches;
Ae night they're mad wi' drink an' whoring,
Niest day their life is past enduring.

    The ladies arm-in-arm in clusters,
As great an' gracious a' as sisters;   220
But hear their absent thoughts o' ither,
They're a' run deils an' jads thegither.
Whyles, owre the wee bit cup an' platie,
They sip the scandal-potion pretty;
Or lee-lang nights, wi' crabbit leuks   225
Pore owre the devil's pictur'd beuks;

232 *gloamin:* dusk
233 *bum-clock:* beetle
234 *kye:* cattle
  rowtin i' the loan: lowing in the lane
235 *gat:* got
  lugs: ears

✦ *Activities*

1 A simple plan for the poem would have been for Burns to make Luath attack the gentry and Caesar defend them, but Burns doesn't do this. To get a grip on the content of the poem, summarise each speech by each dog in three sentences at most.

2 Pick out what you consider to be the emotional climaxes of the poem.

3 Much eighteenth-century satire (see page 170) works by showing an outsider's reactions to aspects of British society, for instance observations by a fictitious Chinese visitor to England. How does Burns create something of the same situation in this poem?

4 How does Burns use the animal nature of the dogs to set an example of behaviour to human beings?

5 If two pets from your street held a backyard conversation about the neighbouring families, what would they be saying? Use Burns's verse form – four iambic feet to each line, in rhyming couplets. See pages 178–179.

6 You are a modern TV producer. You are making a programme for secondary schools about social conditions in eighteenth-century Scotland. Write the storyboard and script (dialogue and voice-over) for a part of it, using this poem as a source. Read selected parts of the poem into your video.

Stake on a chance a farmer's stackyard,
An' cheat like onie unhang'd blackguard.

    There's some exceptions, man an' woman;
But this is Gentry's life in common.   230

    By this, the sun was out o' sight,
An' darker gloamin brought the night;
The bum-clock humm'd wi' lazy drone;
The kye stood rowtin i' the loan;
When up they gat, an' shook their lugs,   235
Rejoic'd they were na *men*, but *dogs*;
An' each took aff his several way,
Resolv'd to meet some ither day.

Notes on 'Address to the Deil'

Background

Most country people and the more extreme Calvinists of the church believed unquestioningly in the Devil and the power of witches in league with him. (See page 165.) John Milton (1608–1674), the English poet, also believed in the Devil as a fallen angel and gave him an impressive role in his long poem *Paradise Lost* (1667), part of which tells of Satan's rebellion and war against God and his ejection from Heaven. By quoting from it, Burns invites comparison between Milton's Satan and the concept of Satan voiced by his own rustic persona.

Verse form

Standard Habbie (see page 180).

---

2 *Hornie:* The Devil was supposed to appear most commonly as a goat, with horns.
Clootie: cloven hooved

3 *cavern:* Hell, usually thought of as below ground

5 *Spairges:* splashes *brunstane:* brimstone
cootie: bowl

6 *scaud:* scald

7 *Hangie:* hangman

11 *skelp:* slap
Skelp and *squeel* are associated with the punishment of the trivial offences of children.

15 *lowin heugh:* flaming pit

17 *lag:* backward

18 *blate:* bashful *scaur:* scared

19 *Whyles:* sometimes. This line strikes a serious note by echoing the Bible: 1 Peter 5, verse 8: *Be sober, be vigilant; because your adversary, the devil, as a roaring lion, walketh about, seeking whom he may devour.*

22 *Till in the kirks:* unroofing the churches. This suggests the storm-raising powers of witches. How does Burns combine dissimilar concepts in this verse?

Address to the Deil

> O Prince! O Chief of many thronèd pow'rs!
> That led th' embattl'd seraphim to war.
>
> Milton.

O thou! whatever title suit thee —
Auld Hornie, Satan, Nick, or Clootie —
Wha in yon cavern grim an' sootie,
        Clos'd under hatches,
Spairges about the brunstane cootie,   5
        To scaud poor wretches!

Hear me, Auld Hangie, for a wee,
An' let poor damnèd bodies be;
I'm sure sma' pleasure it can gie,
        Ev'n to a deil,   10
To skelp an' scaud poor dogs like me
        An' hear us squeel!

Great is thy pow'r an' great thy fame;
Far kend an' noted is thy name;
An' tho' yon lowin heugh's thy hame,   15
        Thou travels far;
An' faith! thou's neither lag, nor lame,
        Nor blate, nor scaur.

Whyles, ranging like a roarin lion,
For prey, a' holes an' corners trying;   20
Whyles, on the strong-wing'd tempest flyin,
        Tirlin the kirks;
Whyles, in the human bosom pryin,
        Unseen thou lurks.

30 *eldritch:*   unearthly

32 *douce:*   decent

33 *yont:*   beyond

35 *boortrees:*   elder bushes

38 *sklentin:*   slanting

41 *rash-buss:*   clump of rushes. Note how Burns ensures that in his own supposed experience he encounters only phenomena which have very ordinary explanations.

42 *sugh:*   moan

43 *nieve:*   fist

45 *stoor:*   hoarse

47 *squatter'd:*   fluttered. The devil could transform himself into any shape, most often an animal.

49–66 All these allegations occur in the records of witch trials throughout Europe for the previous 300 years. The last claim is that witches caused male sexual impotence.

50 *ragweed:*   ragwort

54 *howkit:*   dug up

I've heard my rev'rend graunie say,   25
In lanely glens ye like to stray;
Or, where auld ruin'd castles grey
           Nod to the moon,
Ye fright the nightly wand'rer's way
           Wi' eldritch croon.   30

When twilight did my graunie summon,
To say her pray'rs, douce, honest woman!
Aft yont the dyke she's heard you bummin,
           Wi' eerie drone;
Or, rustlin, thro' the boortrees comin,   35
           Wi' heavy groan.

Ae dreary, windy, winter night,
The stars shot down wi' sklentin light,
Wi' you, mysel, I gat a fright:
           Ayont the lough,   40
Ye, like a rash-buss, stood in sight,
           Wi' waving sugh.

The cudgel in my nieve did shake,
Each bristl'd hair stood like a stake;
When wi' an eldritch, stoor 'quaick, quaick',   45
           Amang the springs,
Awa ye squatter'd like a drake,
           On whistling wings.

Let warlocks grim, an' wither'd hags,
Tell how wi' you, on ragweed nags,   50
They skim the muirs an' dizzy crags,
           Wi' wicked speed;
And in kirk-yards renew their leagues,
           Owre howkit dead.

55 *countra:*   country

56 *kirn:*   butter churn

59 *dawtit:*   petted

   twal-pint hawkie's gaen: twelve-pint cow has gone

60 *yell's the bill:*   dry as the bull

62 *guidmen:*   husbands

   croose: confident

63 *work-lume:*   tool

64 *cantraip wit:*   magic ingenuity

66 *at the bit:*   when at the crucial moment

67 *thowes:*   thaws

   hoord: hoard

68 *icy boord:*   surface

69 In Scottish folklore, a *kelpie* was a form of malign water spirit, a fierce beast in the shape of a horse which lurked in rivers and drowned human beings.

73 *moss:*   bog

   spunkies: will-o'-the-wisps, marsh gas

79–84 Burns is voicing the lurid suspicions of ignorant outsiders as to what goes on in the secret meetings of Masons. There was a secret word that Masons used and a special handshake to identify themselves. As a keen Mason himself, of course, Burns knew that they neither raised storms nor made animal sacrifices.

81 *maun:*   must

83 *brother:*   a member of the Masons

84 *straught:*   straight

Thence, countra wives, wi' toil an' pain,   55
May plunge an' plunge the kirn in vain;
For O! the yellow treasure's taen
        By witching skill;
An' dawtit, twal-pint hawkie's gaen
        As yell's the bill.   60

Thence, mystic knots mak great abuse
On young guidmen, fond, keen an' croose;
When the best wark-lume i' the house,
        By cantraip wit,
Is instant made no worth a louse,   65
        Just at the bit.

When thowes dissolve the snawy hoord,
An' float the jinglin icy boord,
Then, water-kelpies haunt the foord,
        By your direction,   70
An' nighted trav'llers are allur'd
        To their destruction.

And aft your moss-traversing spunkies
Decoy the wight that late an' drunk is:
The bleezin, curst, mischievous monkies   75
        Delude his eyes,
Till in some miry slough he sunk is,
        Ne'er mair to rise.

When Masons' mystic word an' grip
In storms an' tempests raise you up,   80
Some cock or cat your rage maun stop,
        Or, strange to tell!
The youngest brother ye wad whip
        Aff straught to hell.

85–96 Compare this passage with the corresponding passage in the *Paradise Lost* extract (pages 150–151). Which words are most important in conveying Burns's view?

85 *Lang syne:* long ago *yard:* garden

86 *lovers:* Adam and Eve

89 *swaird:* sward, turf

91 *snick-drawing:* latch-lifting. Is Satan here depicted as a Peeping Tom, creeping up on the naked lovers?

92 *incog:* incognito. The Devil was in disguise when he approached Eve in the form of a snake.

93 The *brogue* (trick) was that the Devil persuaded Eve to eat the fruit that God had specifically forbidden.

95 *shog:* shake

96 *'Maist:* almost

97 *bizz:* bustle

98 *reekit duds:* smoky clothes
reestit gizz: scorched wig
Reestit has the definite connotation of smoking fish or ham. (See also 'Tam o' Shanter', page 107 line 202: *In hell they'll roast thee like a herrin!*)

99 *smoulie:* smutty

101 *sklented:* cast

97–108 The *man of Uzz* is Job, whose story may be read in the Bible in The Book of Job. Satan presented himself in Heaven (*'Mang better folk*) and challenged God to let him test Job's allegiance to God by afflicting him with suffering and troubles. Job's wife is the *wicked scaul*, who urged him to *curse God and die.*

107 *lows'd:* loosed *scaul:* scold

108 *warst ava:* worst of all

110 *fechtin:* fighting

111 The archangel Michael, according to legend and Milton's *Paradise Lost*, Book Six, lines 323–327, was responsible for wounding Satan in the battle of the loyal angels against the angels who rebelled against God.

113 *ding:* beat *Lallan:* Lowland
Erse: Gaelic (originally Irish)

Lang syne in Eden's bonie yard,   85
When youthfu' lovers first were pair'd,
An' all the soul of love they shar'd,
        The raptur'd hour,
Sweet on the fragrant flow'ry swaird,
        In shady bow'r: 90

Then you, ye auld, snick-drawing dog!
Ye cam to Paradise incog,
An' play'd on man a cursed brogue
        (Black be your fa'!),
An' gied the infant warld a shog,   95
        'Maist ruin'd a'.

D'ye mind that day when in a bizz
Wi' reekit duds, an' reestit gizz,
Ye did present your smoutie phiz
        'Mang better folk;   100
An' sklented on the man of Uzz
        Your spitefu' joke?

An' how ye gat him i' your thrall,
An' brak him out o' house an' hal',
While scabs an' botches did him gall,   105
        Wi' bitter claw;
An' lows'd his ill-tongu'd, wicked scaul—
        Was warst ava?

But a' your doings to rehearse,
Your wily snares an' fechtin fierce,   110
Sin' that day Michael* did you pierce
        Down to this time,
Wad ding a Lallan tongue, or Erse,
        In prose or rhyme.

116 *rantin:*   roistering
119 *jinkin:*   dodging
122 *men':*   mend your ways
123 *aiblins:*   perhaps
124 *stake:*   chance
123–124 Burns is suggesting that even the Devil might not be beyond redemption if he just exercised his free will.
125 *wae:*   woeful

✦ *Activities*

1 To get a better grip on its subject matter, try dividing up the poem into three sections, with the following headings:
   - An invocation to the devil
   - A catalogue of the devil's activities
     - in Scotland
     - in the Bible
   - The poet's own relationship with the devil.

2 How does Burns establish the tone of his poem – his attitude to the subject? Consider: the choice of the Scots language, his use of the persona or role he writes in, the parallels to the Bible and to *Paradise Lost*.

3 Explain how this poem is at the same time both funny and a serious statement of a standpoint in a religious debate.

4 After his death, having been turned back at the Pearly Gates of Heaven, Burns comes knocking at the door of Hell. Improvise and tape record a discussion between him and the Devil.

An' now, Auld Cloots, I ken ye're thinkin,   115
A certain Bardie's rantin, drinkin,
Some luckless hour will send him linkin
          To your black Pit;
But, faith! he'll turn a corner jinkin,
          An' cheat you yet.   120

But fare-you-weel, Auld Nickie-Ben!
O, wad ye tak a thought an' men'!
Ye aiblins might—I dinna ken—
          Still hae a stake:
I'm wae to think upo' yon den,   125
          Ev'n for your sake!

* *Michael:* vide *Milton, Book 6th* [Robert Burns's own note]

Notes on 'Auld lang syne'

Verse form
Ballad metre: tetrameter and trimeter lines rhyming abcb.

---

   4 *auld lang syne:* old long ago. This phrase was widely current in Scots songs before Burns's time.

   5 *dear:* Other versions of the three extant have *jo*, a friend, possibly male.

   7 *cup o' kindness:* a drink in which lovers pledge their love

   9 *be:* buy
      stoup: tankard

 13 *braes:* hillsides

 14 *gowans:* daisies

 15 *fit:* foot, step

 18 *dine:* dinner

 19 *braid:* broad

 21 *fiere:* comrade

 22 *gie's:* give me

 23 *gude-willie-waught:* good-will drink pledging loyalty

✦ *Activities*

1 What seems to be the history of the friendship between the two people (*we twa*) in the poem, speaker and spoken to?

2 What would be wrong with swapping round the second halves of stanzas 3 and 4?

3 Throughout the world this is sung as a song of parting. It can also be regarded as a song of reunion; a drinking song; a song of reminiscence; a communal song; an individual's song; a song of companionship; a love song; a song of regret.
   What elements seem most important?

Auld lang syne

TUNE: *Auld lang syne*

Should auld acquaintance be forgot
    And never brought to mind?
Should auld acquaintance be forgot,
    And auld lang syne!

    Chorus
For auld lang syne, my dear,   5
    For auld lang syne,
We'll tak' a cup o' kindness yet,
    For auld lang syne.

And surely ye'll be your pint-stoup,
    And surely I'll be mine!   10
And we'll tak' a cup o' kindness yet,
    For auld lang syne.

We twa hae run about the braes,
    And pu'd the gowans fine;
But we've wander'd mony a weary fit,   15
    Sin' auld lang syne.

We twa hae paidl'd in the burn,
    Frae morning sun till dine;
But seas between us braid hae roar'd,
    Sin' auld lang syne.   20

And there's a hand, my trusty fiere!
    And gie's a hand o' thine!
And we'll tak a right gude-willie-waught,
    For auld lang syne.

Notes on 'I hae a wife o' my ain'

Background
In 1788 Burns was married at last to Jean Armour (see page 157) and installed in the farm at Ellisland near Dumfries (see page 158). The tune was previously associated with some old verses on the same theme.

Verse form
Four-line verses of trimeter, rhyming abab.

---

2 *partake:* share

3 & 4 *Cuckold:* A cuckold is a man whose wife has committed adultery.

11 *guid braid:* good broad

12 *dunts:* blows

✦ *Activities*

1 How does the philosophy of this poem compare with the ideas expressed in 'For a' that and a' that' on page 121?

2 Write a short story in which this man's character is shown by one incident. A second incident either confirms his character or changes it.

   Set the action at any time and place of your choosing. Decide whether your character will be seen entirely from the outside or whether you will be able to reveal his inner thoughts and feelings.

   Your story is to be submitted to a general interest magazine which publishes one short story in each issue along with articles on a wide range of subjects.

I hae a wife o' my ain

TUNE: *I hae a wife o' my ain*

I hae a wife o' my ain,
    I'll partake wi' naebody;
I'll tak Cuckold frae nane,
    I'll gie Cuckold to naebody.

I hae a penny to spend—   5
    There—thanks to naebody;
I hae naething to lend,
    I'll borrow frae naebody.

I am naebody's lord,
    I'll be slave to naebody;
I hae a guid braid sword,   10
    I'll tak dunts frae naebody.

I'll be merry and free,
    I'll be sad for naebody;
Naebody cares for me,   15
    I care for naebody.

Notes on 'Yestreen I had a pint o' wine'

Background
This was written during Burns's affair with Anne Park, barmaid and niece of an innkeeper in Dumfries. A daughter was born in March, 1791, nine days before Jean Armour Burns bore Robert Burns a son. Jean brought up Anne's child in the Burns family.

Verse form
Ballad metre: tetrameter and trimeter lines, but rhyming abab.

---

1   *Yestreen:*   yesterday evening
4   *gowden:*   golden
6   *manna:*   In the Bible, the people of Israel when wandering in the desert after escaping from slavery in Egypt were fed by God with food dropped from Heaven. See Exodus 16, verses 11–15.
7   *hiney:*   honey
10   *Indus:*   a river in north India
Savannah: a river and town in Georgia, USA
11   *Gie:*   give
14   *Sultana:*   the wife of a sultan
15   *dying raptures:*   Death is a frequent poetic euphemism for sexual fulfilment.
17   *God of Day:*   the sun
18   *Diana:*   the moon in classical Roman mythology
19   *Ilk:*   each

Yestreen I had a pint o' wine

TUNE: *Banks of Banna*

Yestreen I had a pint o' wine,
   A place where body saw na;
Yestreen lay on this breast o' mine
   The gowden locks of Anna.

The hungry Jew in wilderness   5
   Rejoicing o'er his manna
Was naething to my hiney bliss
   Upon the lips of Anna.

Ye monarchs take the East and West
   Frae Indus to Savannah: 10
Gie me within my straining grasp
   The melting form of Anna!

There I'll despise Imperial charms,
   An Empress or Sultana,
While dying raptures in her arms   15
   I give and take wi' Anna!

Awa, thou flaunting God of Day!
   Awa, thou pale Diana!
Ilk Star, gae hide thy twinkling ray,
   When I'm to meet my Anna!   20

Come, in thy raven plumage, Night
   (Sun, Moon, and Stars, withdrawn a'),
And bring an Angel-pen to write
   My transports with my Anna!

25 *Kirk:*   the Church of Scotland, established by law as the national church

26 *maunna:*   must not

29 *e'e:*   eye

30 *but:*   without

31 *but:*   only

✦ *Activities*

1 Compare this poem with 'A red red Rose' (page 119). How does the poet's attitude to the two women differ and how does the choice of imagery and types of language in each poem convey these attitudes?

2 Burns wrote of this poem, 'I think [it] is the best love-song I ever composed in my life; but in its *original* state it is not quite a lady's song.' What does Burns mean by 'a lady's song'? After reading the love songs in this selection, do you agree with his verdict?

3 Imagine that Betty Paton, mother of Burns's first 'Bastart Wean' five years earlier (see page 16), has heard of his infatuation with Anne Park, and someone has passed her a handwritten copy of this poem. Write Betty's letter to Anne, care of the Globe Inn, Dumfries, giving her advice. Date it July, 1790, before Anne became pregnant.

   You might also like to write Anne's reply.

Postscript

The Kirk an' State may join, and tell   25
    To do sic things I maunna:
The Kirk an' State may gae to Hell,
    And I'll gae to my Anna.

She is the sunshine o' my e'e,
    To live but her I canna: 30
Had I on earth but wishes three,
    The first should be my Anna.

Notes on 'Tam o' Shanter'

Background
Captain Francis Grose, an Englishman who was writing a 'guidebook' to Scotland, asked Burns to supply a poem to accompany a description of Alloway Kirk. Burns said that the story was 'authentic' and based on local tradition (see page 153).

   The mock epic elements (see page 171) in the poem probably arise from Burns's reading of Pope's translations of Homer's epics (see extract, page 154).

Verse form
Octosyllabic rhyming couplets.

The epigraph
From the *Prologue* to Book VI of *The Aeneid* by Virgil, translated into Scots by Gavin Douglas (1474–1522).

---

   1 *chapman billies:*   pedlar fellows
   2 *drouthy:*   thirsty
   4 *gate:*   road
   5 *nappy:*   ale
   6 *fou:* drunk   *unco:*   very
   7 *lang Scots miles:*   Burns depicts his narrator and his old-fashioned Ayrshire community as still thinking in terms of the Scots measures used in the independent state which was abolished in 1707. A Scots mile was about 1810 metres and thus longer than the imperial mile of 1609 metres used throughout the UK today.
   8 *mosses, waters, slaps:*   peat cuttings, streams, gaps in walls
  13 *fand:*   found
  18 *taen:* taken   *ain:*   own
  19 *skellum:*   rogue
  20 *blethering:* chattering   *blellum:*   babbler
  22 *Ae:*   at every
  23 *ilka melder:*   each meal-grinding

Tam o' Shanter
A Tale

Of Brownyis and of Bogillis full is this Buke.
Gawin Douglas.

When chapman billies leave the street,
And drouthy neebors neebors meet;
As market-days are wearing late,
An' folk begin to tak the gate;
While we sit bousing at the nappy,   5
An' getting fou and unco happy,
We think na on the lang Scots miles,
The mosses, waters, slaps, and styles,
That lie between us and our hame,
Whare sits our sulky, sullen dame,   10
Gathering her brows like gathering storm,
Nursing her wrath to keep it warm.

    This truth fand honest Tam o' Shanter,
As he frae Ayr ae night did canter:
(Auld Ayr, wham ne'er a town surpasses,   15
For honest men and bonie lasses).

    O Tam, had'st thou but been sae wise,
As taen thy ain wife Kate's advice!
She tauld thee weel thou was a skellum,
A blethering, blustering, drunken blellum;   20
That frae November till October,
Ae market-day thou was nae sober;
That ilka melder, wi' the miller,

24 *siller:* money

25 *naig was ca'd a shoe on:* nag that had a shoe nailed on

30 *Doon:* the river between Alloway and Shanter farm

31 *warlocks in the mirk:* wizards in the darkness

32 *Alloway's auld haunted kirk:* The church had been abandoned in 1756 and swiftly became ruinous. Burns had grown up not far from it for his first seven years and must have known it well.

33 *gars me greet:* makes me weep

35 By this point in the poem, what expectations has Burns raised in his reader?

40 *reaming swats:* frothing ale

41 *Souter:* cobbler

51 *rair:* roar

53 *Care:* The personification of an abstraction like this is a typical device of the elevated style of much 18th-century poetry. Read line 54 and note Burns's ironic use of it here.

Thou sat as lang as thou had siller;
That ev'ry naig was ca'd a shoe on,   25
The smith and thee gat roaring fou on;
That at the Lord's house, even on Sunday,
Thou drank wi' Kirkton Jean till Monday.
She prophesied that, late or soon,
Thou would be found deep drown'd in Doon,   30
Or catch'd wi' warlocks in the mirk
By Alloway's auld haunted kirk.

    Ah, gentle dames! it gars me greet,
To think how monie counsels sweet,
How monie lengthen'd sage advices   35
The husband frae the wife despises!

    But to our tale:—Ae market-night,
Tam had got planted unco right,
Fast by an ingle, bleezing finely,
Wi' reaming swats that drank divinely;   40
And at his elbow, Souter Johnie,
His ancient, trusty, drouthy cronie:
Tam lo'ed him like a vera brither;
They had been fou for weeks thegither.
The night drave on wi' sangs and clatter;   45
And ay the ale was growing better:
The landlady and Tam grew gracious,
Wi' favours, secret, sweet and precious:
The Souter tauld his queerest stories;
The landlord's laugh was ready chorus: 50
The storm without might rair and rustle,
Tam did na mind the storm a whistle.

    Care, mad to see a man sae happy,
E'en drown'd himsel amang the nappy.

55 *bees:*   Bees produce honey and stings. Note and read on for the next reference to bees.
lades: loads

59–66 Critics debate the significance of these lines. The language is not only English but rather literary English. An expression like *the borealis race* is a typical 18th-century poetic circumlocution, a roundabout and supposedly more dignified way of referring to something. *Evanishing* is more used in earlier Scots literature than in English. What effect do you think these lines have in the context of the poem as a whole?

71 *sic:*   such

73 *'twad:*   it would have

81 *skelpit:*   dashed
dub: puddle

83 *Whiles:*   sometimes

85 *glow'ring:*   staring

As bees flee hame wi' lades o' treasure,   55
The minutes wing'd their way wi' pleasure:
Kings may be blest, but Tam was glorious,
O'er a' the ills o' life victorious!

But pleasures are like poppies spread:
You seize the flow'r, its bloom is shed;   60
Or like the snow falls in the river,
A moment white—then melts for ever;
Or like the borealis race,
That flit ere you can point their place;
Or like the rainbow's lovely form   65
Evanishing amid the storm.
Nae man can tether time or tide;
The hour approaches Tam maun ride:
That hour, o' night's black arch the key-stane,
That dreary hour he mounts his beast in;   70
And sic a night he taks the road in,
As ne'er poor sinner was abroad in.

The wind blew as 'twad blawn its last;
The rattling showers rose on the blast;
The speedy gleams the darkness swallow'd;   75
Loud, deep, and lang the thunder bellow'd:
That night, a child might understand,
The Deil had business on his hand.

Weel mounted on his gray mare Meg,
A better never lifted leg,   80
Tam skelpit on thro' dub and mire,
Despising wind, and rain, and fire;
Whiles holding fast his guid blue bonnet,
Whiles crooning o'er some auld Scots sonnet,
Whiles glow'ring round wi' prudent cares,   85

86 *bogles:* hobgoblins

88 *houlets:* owls

89–97 It is claimed that all these details were or are still identifiable on a route from Ayr to Alloway. This is possible as Burns must have roamed the area as a child. He was evidently drawing on childhood memories of tales told to him by his mother's old servant, Betty Davidson, while he was still living in his birthplace at Alloway.

90 *smoor'd:* smothered

91 *birks:* birches
meikle: huge

93 *whins:* furze

94 *fand:* found

95 *aboon:* above

103 *ilka bore:* every cranny

105 *John Barleycorn:* A personification of barley as the grain from which both ale and whisky are made. Burns wrote a poem called 'John Barleycorn, a ballad' which was an adaptation of a traditional folksong about the life cycle of barley from sowing to brewing and boozing.

107 *tippeny:* ale

108 *usquabae:* whisky

109 *swats sae ream'd:* new beer bubbled so much

110 If they would only fight fairly, he cared not a farthing for devils.

114 *unco:* wondrous

114–218 Every detail reflects Burns's intimate knowledge of the accusations made in witch trials and the beliefs of self-styled 'witches', who sometimes seem to have been as credulous as their accusers. (See page 165.)

116 *cotillion:* the name for a group of dances of French origin for four or eight dancers, perhaps regarded as especially wicked by the Calvinist anti-dancing faction
brent brand

Lest bogles catch him unawares:
Kirk-Alloway was drawing nigh,
Whare ghaists and houlets nightly cry.

   By this time he was cross the ford,
Whare in the snaw the chapman smoor'd;   90
And past the birks and meikle stane,
Whare drunken Charlie brak's neck-bane;
And thro' the whins, and by the cairn,
Whare hunters fand the murder'd bairn;
And near the thorn, aboon the well,   95
Whare Mungo's mither hang'd hersel.—
Before him Doon pours all his floods;
The doubling storm roars thro' the woods;
The lightnings flash from pole to pole;
Near and more near the thunders roll: 100
When, glimmering thro' the groaning trees,
Kirk-Alloway seem'd in a bleeze;
Thro' ilka bore the beams were glancing,
And loud resounded mirth and dancing.

   Inspiring bold John Barleycorn,   105
What dangers thou canst make us scorn!
Wi' tippeny, we fear nae evil;
Wi' usquabae, we'll face the Devil!—
The swats sae ream'd in Tammie's noddle,
Fair play, he car'd na deils a boddle.   110
But Maggie stood, right sair astonish'd,
Till, by the heel and hand admonish'd,
She ventur'd forward on the light;
And, vow! Tam saw an unco sight!
Warlocks and witches in a dance: 115
Nae cotillion, brent new frae France,

117 These dances are homely Scottish ones, contrasting with the devilish image of witchcraft.

119 *winnock-bunker:* window seat

121 *towsie tyke:* shaggy dog

123 *gart:* made
skirl: shrill

124 *dirl:* rattle

125 *presses:* cupboards

127 *cantraip slight:* weird trick

130 *the haly table:* the communion table, the Protestant equivalent of the altar, the most revered part of the church, where the sacrament of communion or mass is performed

131 *banes, in gibbet-airns:* After some executions, the body of the criminal was exposed in an iron cage hanging from a gibbet at some public place, such as a crossroads, until it disintegrated, no doubt to act as a warning to others.

133 *rape:* rope

134 *gab:* mouth

135/136 *tomahawks* and *scymitars:* exotic weapons from far-off countries, perhaps hinting how far the witches can travel by supernatural means provided by the Devil, broomsticks, etc.

137 Witches were supposed to use the body parts of unbaptised babies and criminals in their spells.

140 *stack to the heft:* stuck to the haft

143 *glowr'd:* stared

147 *cleekit:* linked arms

148 *ilka carlin swat and reekit:* each witch sweated and steamed

149 *coost her duddies:* cast off her rags

150 *linket at it:* skipped along
sark: chemise

But hornpipes, jigs, strathspeys, and reels,
Put life and mettle in their heels.
A winnock-bunker in the east,
There sat Auld Nick, in shape o' beast;   120
A towsie tyke, black, grim, and large,
To gie them music was his charge:
He screw'd the pipes and gart them skirl,
Till roof and rafters a' did dirl.
Coffins stood round, like open presses,   125
That shaw'd the dead in their last dresses;
And, by some devilish cantraip slight,
Each in its cauld hand held a light:
By which heroic Tam was able
To note upon the haly table,   130
A murderer's banes, in gibbet-airns;
Twa span-lang, wee, unchristen'd bairns;
A thief, new-cutted frae a rape—
Wi' his last gasp his gab did gape;
Five tomahawks wi' bluid red-rusted;   135
Five scymitars wi' murder crusted;
A garter which a babe had strangled;
A knife a father's throat had mangled—
Whom his ain son o' life bereft—
The grey hairs yet stack to the heft;   140
Wi' mair o' horrible and awefu',
Which even to name wad be unlawfu'.

   As Tammie glowr'd, amaz'd, and curious,
The mirth and fun grew fast and furious;
The piper loud and louder blew,   145
The dancers quick and quicker flew,
They reel'd, they set, they cross'd, they cleekit,
Till ilka carlin swat and reekit,
And coost her duddies to the wark,
And linket at it in her sark!   150

151 *thae:* these
   queans: girls
153 *creeshie flannen:* greasy flannel
154 *seventeen hunder linen:* fine linen woven to a particular standard. The use of this phrase may have come to Burns from his six months as a flax-dresser at Irvine (1781–1782).
155 *Thir:* these
157 *hurdies:* buttocks
158 *ae blink:* one glimpse
   burdies: lassies
155–158 How does this outburst affect your view of the character of the narrator? What else do you learn about him from other parts of the poem?
160 *Rigwoodie:* gnarled
   wad spean: would disgust
161 *Louping:* leaping
   crummock: staff
163 *fu' brawlie:* very well
164 *wawlie:* choice
165 *core:* company
169 *meikle:* much *bear:* barley
171 *cutty sark:* short chemise
   Paisley harn: coarse cloth
174 *vauntie:* proud
176 *coft:* bought
177 *twa pund Scots:* Scots pounds were officially abolished in 1707 with the end of the independent kingdom. They were then worth about one twelfth of an English pound sterling. People continued to use the term well into Burns's time.

Now Tam, O Tam! had thae been queans,
A' plump and strapping in their teens!
Their sarks, instead o' creeshie flannen,
Been snaw-white seventeen hunder linen!—
Thir breeks o' mine, my only pair,   155
That ance were plush, o' guid blue hair,
I wad hae gi'en them off my hurdies
For ae blink o' the bonie burdies!

But wither'd beldams, auld and droll,
Rigwoodie hags wad spean a foal,   160
Louping and flinging on a crummock,
I wonder did na turn thy stomach!

But Tam kend what was what fu' brawlie:
There was ae winsome wench and wawlie,
That night enlisted in the core,   165
Lang after kend on Carrick shore
(For monie a beast to dead she shot,
An' perish'd monie a bonie boat,
And shook baith meikle corn and bear,
And kept the country-side in fear).   170
Her cutty sark, o' Paisley harn,
That while a lassie she had worn,
In longitude tho' sorely scanty,
It was her best, and she was vauntie.—
Ah! little kend thy reverend grannie,   175
That sark she coft for her wee Nannie,
Wi' twa pund Scots ('twas a' her riches),
Wad ever grac'd a dance of witches!

179 *Muse:* An 18th-century poetic convention implying that the poet's inspiration comes from a spirit like an angel (hence *wing*). If your muse can fly high you can successfully attempt great subjects in your poetry.
cour: stoop

181 *lap and flang:* leaped and high kicked

182 *jad:* a word of abuse for a woman (a jade, or worn-out horse)

185 *Satan:* a Hebrew biblical name for the Devil
glowr'd, and fidg'd fu' fain: stared, and twitched with desire

186 *hotch'd:* jerked up and down

187 *ae caper, syne anither:* one leap, then another

188 *tint:* lost

193 *fyke:* fret

194 *herds:* shepherds
byke: hive

195 *open pussie's:* bay the hare's

193–200 *As ... As ... As ... So:* This passage imitates the epic similes used by Homer and Virgil. Compare the tone of these lines with the extract from *The Iliad* on page 154.

200 *eldritch:* unearthly
hollo: yell

201 *fairin:* deserts

202 *herrin:* herring. What effect was Burns seeking when he chose this simile?

206 *key-stane:* the central stone of an arch

210 *fient:* devil

But here my Muse her wing maun cour;
Sic flights are far beyond her power: 180
To sing how Nannie lap and flang
(A souple jad she was, and strang),
And how Tam stood like ane bewitch'd,
And thought his very een enrich'd;
Even Satan glowr'd, and fidg'd fu' fain,   185
And hotch'd and blew wi' might and main;
Till first ae caper, syne anither,
Tam tint his reason a' thegither,
And roars out: 'Weel done, Cutty-sark!'
And in an instant all was dark;   190
And scarcely had he Maggie rallied,
When out the hellish legion sallied.

As bees bizz out wi' angry fyke,
When plundering herds assail their byke;
As open pussie's mortal foes,   195
When, pop! she starts before their nose;
As eager runs the market-crowd,
When 'Catch the thief!' resounds aloud:
So Maggie runs, the witches follow,
Wi' monie an eldritch skreech and hollo.   200

Ah, Tam! Ah, Tam! thou'll get thy fairin!
In hell they'll roast thee like a herrin!
In vain thy Kate awaits thy comin!
Kate soon will be a woefu' woman!
Now, do thy speedy utmost, Meg,   205
And win the key-stane* of the brig;
There, at them thou thy tail may toss,
A running stream they dare na cross!
But ere the key-stane she could make,
The fient a tail she had to shake;   210
For Nannie, far before the rest,

213 *ettle:* intent
215 *hale:* whole
217 *carlin claught:* witch clutched
220 *ilk:* each

✦ *Activities*

1 Draw a graph showing how tension or excitement rises and falls in the course of this tale. The vertical axis should show the degree of tension or excitement. The horizontal axis should show the progress of events. Label each event.

2 Tam is portrayed intimately from the inside as someone supposedly very much like an ordinary person but also from the outside as a caricature. How does the poem achieve this effect?

3 The character of the narrator is very important in determining how readers regard the events of the tale. Start from the work you did in response to the note at lines 155–158 and discuss who the narrator is and how the tone of his voice changes. Prepare parts of the poem for a public reading or make a tape recording.

4 Explain the ways in which this poem is humorous.

5 Imagine that you are a reader of the *Edinburgh Herald* and you have read 'Tam o' Shanter' in the issue of 18 March 1791. You are deeply offended by it. Write a letter to the Editor protesting at the publishing of such a poem. (You will need to decide what kind of people Burns's satire was attacking and exactly how the poem would offend them.)

Hard upon noble Maggie prest,
And flew at Tam wi' furious ettle;
But little wist she Maggie's mettle!
Ae spring brought off her master hale,   215
But left behind her ain grey tail:
The carlin claught her by the rump,
And left poor Maggie scarce a stump.

   Now, wha this tale o' truth shall read,
Ilk man and mother's son, take heed: 220
Whene'er to drink you are inclin'd,
Or cutty sarks run in your mind,
Think! ye may buy the joys o'er dear:
Remember Tam o' Shanter's mare.

*   *It is a well known fact that witches, or any evil spirits, have no power to follow a poor wight any farther than the middle of the next running stream.— It may be proper likewise to mention to the benighted traveller, that when he falls in with bogles, whatever danger may be in his going forward, there is much more hazard in turning back.* [Robert Burns's note]

Notes on 'John Anderson my Jo'

Background
This poem is based on an older song going back to 1560, and more immediately on a bawdy version in *The Merry Muses of Caledonia*, which was printed only after Burns's death (see page 155).

Verse form
Ballad metre, but arranged in eight-line stanzas to fit the tune, which goes back to the 17th century.

---

1 *jo:* dear
4 *brent:* smooth
5 *beld:* bald
7 *pow:* head
10 *thegither:* together
11 *canty:* cheerful
13 *maun:* must

✦ *Activities*

1 Who speaks this poem and to whom? Write a short article for their local newspaper about this well-known couple after the death of the second of them.

2 Study the details of the extended metaphor in stanza 2. Discuss:
- what it really refers to;
- what feelings are expressed by using it;
- how different interpretations of the second last line might add to or detract from the effect of the song.

3 How do the figures of speech and the language used give a character to the speaker?

John Anderson my Jo

TUNE: *John Anderson my jo, John*

John Anderson my jo, John,
   When we were first acquent;
Your locks were like the raven,
   Your bonie brow was brent;
But now your brow is beld, John,   5
   Your locks are like the snaw;
But blessings on your frosty pow,
   John Anderson my jo.

John Anderson my jo, John,
   We clamb the hill thegither;   10
And mony a canty day, John,
   We've had wi' ane anither:
Now we maun totter down, John,
   And hand in hand we'll go;
And sleep thegither at the foot,   15
   John Anderson my jo.

Notes on 'Ae fond kiss'

Background
Burns had met Mrs Agnes McLehose (Nancy), the estranged wife of a West Indian planter, in Edinburgh in 1787 when he was already famous. She and Burns had a passionate but probably platonic affair and finally parted in 1791.

The tune title indicates a Gaelic origin.

Verse form
Tetrameter couplets.

---

3 *pledge thee:*   drink your health
4 *wage:*   promise
9 *partial fancy:*   loving impulse

✦ *Activities*

1 Consider:
   - the metaphors – conventional or original;
   - the use of simple straightforward language;
   - the proportions of exclusively Scots words and of words common to Scots and English.

   Describe the style of this poem in the light of your examination.

2 What feelings are expressed in this poem? For instance, is there any bitterness?

3 All the rhymes in this poem are 'feminine', that is, of two syllables with stress on the first. Try to get hold of the music or a recording of a performance. Listen to how the melody and the rhymes come together to create the emotion of the poem.

4 Both this song and 'A red red Rose' (page 119) are about parting, so why are the emotions so different in each?

Ae fond kiss

TUNE: *Rory Dall's port*

Ae fond kiss, and then we sever;
Ae fareweel, and then—for ever!
Deep in heart-wrung tears I'll pledge thee!
Warring sighs and groans I'll wage thee!

Who shall say that Fortune grieves him,   5
While the star of hope she leaves him?
Me, nae chearfu' twinkle lights me;
Dark despair around benights me.

I'll ne'er blame my partial fancy,
Naething could resist my Nancy: 10
But to see her, was to love her—
Love but her, and love for ever.

Had we never lov'd sae kindly—
Had we never lov'd sae blindly—
Never met—or never parted,   15
We had ne'er been broken-hearted!

Fare thee weel, thou first and fairest!
Fare thee weel, thou best and dearest!
Thine be ilka joy and treasure,
Peace, Enjoyment, Love and Pleasure!   20

Ae fond kiss, and then we sever!
Ae fareweel, alas! for ever!
Deep in heart-wrung tears I'll pledge thee,
Warring sighs and groans I'll wage thee.

Notes on 'Such a parcel of rogues in a nation'

Background
Burns is thinking back to the Union of Parliaments in 1707, when members of the Scottish Parliament were richly bribed to vote for their union with the English Parliament. The refrain was traditional and the tune is early 18th century.

Verse form
Ballad metre: tetrameter and trimeter lines, but rhyming abab.

---

3 The new fashion was to refer to North Britain (see page 161).

5 *Sark:*   This stream marks the Border at its western end.

6 *Tweed:*   The River Tweed marks the Border at its eastern end.

7 *England's province:*   The speaker thinks Scotland has been reduced to a mere province of England by the Union of 1707.

17 *'or:*   before

19 *lien:*   lain

20 *Bruce and loyal Wallace:*   Robert the Bruce (1274–1329), King of Scots, and Sir William Wallace (c1270–1305), heroes of the Scottish War of Independence in the late 13th and early 14th centuries

21 *But pith and power:*   Even though I am without pith and power.

✦ *Activity*
You are a secret agent for the new government in London in 1708. You overhear the speaker of this poem in a pub in Edinburgh. Write a report for your superiors, deducing all you can about his background and level of education. End with an opinion as to how dangerous he is to the new regime.

Such a parcel of rogues in a nation

TUNE: *A parcel of rogues in a nation*

Fareweel to a' our Scottish fame,
　　Fareweel our ancient glory;
Fareweel even to the Scottish name,
　　Sae fam'd in martial story!

Now Sark rins o'er the Solway sands,　　　　　　5
　　And Tweed rins to the ocean,
To mark where England's province stands—
　　Such a parcel of rogues in a nation!

What force or guile could not subdue
　　Thro' many warlike ages,　　　　　　　　　　10
Is wrought now by a coward few,
　　For hireling traitors' wages.

The English steel we could disdain,
　　Secure in valour's station;
But English gold has been our bane—　　　　　　15
　　Such a parcel of rogues in a nation!

O would, 'or I had seen the day
　　That treason thus could sell us,
My auld grey head had lien in clay,
　　Wi' Bruce and loyal Wallace!　　　　　　　　20

But pith and power, till my last hour,
　　I'll mak this declaration,—
We're bought and sold for English gold—
　　Such a parcel of rogues in a nation!

Notes on 'Scots, wha hae'

Background

Burns originally entitled this poem 'Robert Bruce's March to
Bannockburn'. This is partly a genuine celebration of the famous
victory of 1314. But in a letter Burns says he is inspired not only by
Bruce's 'glorious struggle for Freedom' but also by the 'glowing
ideas of some other struggles of the same nature, *not quite so
ancient*'. He was referring to the trial for sedition and the
transportation of the young lawyer Thomas Muir of Huntershill
near Glasgow. He had merely organised a peaceful movement for
parliamentary reform but was taken to London in chains. (See
page 160.)

Verse form

Three rhyming lines of tetrameter and one of trimeter.

---

1 *Wallace:* Sir William Wallace (c1270–1305), who led
   the Scots against the occupation by King Edward I of
   England
2 *Bruce:* Robert the Bruce (1274–1329), crowned King of
   Scots in 1306. He expelled the English occupation
   forces after the victory at Bannockburn.
6 *front o' battle:* the front line of the enemy army

✦ *Activities*

1 What sentiments does Bruce appeal to in his army to
   encourage them to fight? Which is given most importance?

2 Underline any words or phrases which present physical
   experiences. Does this suit the situation?

3 This is a poem of high political drama. What kind of language
   does Burns choose for it? How Scottish, how abstract?

Scots, wha hae

TUNE: *Hey, tuttie taitie*

Scots, wha hae wi' Wallace bled,
Scots, wham Bruce has aften led,
Welcome to your gory bed,
      Or to victory!

Now's the day, and now's the hour;   5
See the front o' battle lour;
See approach proud Edward's power—
      Chains and slavery!

Wha will be a traitor knave?
Wha can fill a coward's grave?   10
Wha sae base as be a slave?
      Let him turn and flee!

Wha for Scotland's king and law
Freedom's sword will strongly draw,
Freeman stand, or freeman fa',   15
      Let him follow me!

By oppression's woes and pains!
By your sons in servile chains!
We will drain our dearest veins,
      But they shall be free!   20

Lay the proud usurpers low!
Tyrants fall in every foe!
Liberty's in every blow!
      Let us do, or die!

Notes on 'A red red Rose'

Background
Based on a folksong original which Burns said he 'pickt up'. Burns said he was 'charmed with it'. He had no tune in mind for the poem and it was linked to its now accepted tune, 'Low down in the Broom', in 1821.

Various phrases can be found in older printed poems, showing how the traditional phrases and images of folksong were reworked by each poet. (See extracts, page 156.)

Verse form
Ballad metre: tetrameter and trimeter lines, rhyming abcb.

---

8 *gang:* go

✦ *Activities*

1 Who is speaking in this poem and what is the situation?

2 Think over the similes used in stanza 1 and describe the impression you gain of the nature of the loved one.

3 Some of the images in this poem are of things that change and pass. Others are of enduring things. Explain how the interplay between the two groups conveys the poet's feelings.

4 There is an element of hyperbole (deliberate exaggeration) in this poem. How suitable is it to the subject matter and how does it suggest the character of the speaker?

5 Practise reading this poem aloud as expressively as you can to a small audience.

A red red Rose

O my luve's like a red, red rose
   That's newly sprung in June;
O my luve's like the melodie
   That's sweetly play'd in tune.

As fair art thou, my bonie lass,   5
   So deep in luve am I;
And I will love thee still, my dear,
   Till a' the seas gang dry.

Till a' the seas gang dry, my dear,
   And the rocks melt wi' the sun: 10
O I will love thee still, my dear,
   While the sands o' life shall run.

And fare thee weel, my only luve!
   And fare thee weel, a while!
And I will come again, my luve,   15
   Tho' 'twere ten thousand mile!

Notes on 'For a' that and a' that'

Background

The French Revolution had been in progress since 1789. In December 1792, when war with France had broken out, an informer denounced Burns to his employers, the Excise Board, as an unpatriotic sympathiser with revolutionary ideas.

The ideas in the poem echo those in *Rights of Man,* a pamphlet issued in two parts in 1791 and 1792 by an English Quaker, Thomas Paine, who had been in the new American republic and 'defected' to revolutionary France (see pages 160 and 166). In the same month of January 1795 in which he wrote this poem, Burns referred to the recently guillotined King and Queen of France as 'a perjured Blockhead and an unprincipled Prostitute' in a letter to his friend, Mrs Dunlop. Universal brotherhood was one of the principles of Freemasonry (see page 165).

The refrain 'For a' that and a' that' was traditional and the tune of that title already existed.

Verse form

Iambic tetrameter, rhyming abab in the first four lines and arranged in eight line stanzas to match the tune.

---

7 *the guinea's stamp:*   the superficial design stamped on to the metal coin

8 *gowd:*   gold

10 *hoddin grey:*   coarse grey woollen cloth

17 *birkie ca'd:*   fellow, called

20 *coof:*   fool

For a' that and a' that

Is there, for honest poverty
   That hangs his head, and a' that?
The coward-slave, we pass him by—
   We dare be poor for a' that!
For a' that, and a' that,   5
   Our toils obscure, and a' that,
The rank is but the guinea's stamp—
   The man's the gowd for a' that.

What though on hamely fare we dine,
   Wear hoddin grey, and a' that?   10
Gie fools their silks, and knaves their wine—
   A man's a man, for a' that:
For a' that, and a' that,
   Their tinsel show, and a' that;
The honest man, though e'er sae poor,   15
   Is king o' men for a' that.

Ye see yon birkie ca'd a lord,
   Wha struts, and stares, and a' that;
Though hundreds worship at his word,
   He's but a coof for a' that: 20
For a' that, and a' that,
   His ribband, star, and a' that,
The man of independent mind,
   He looks and laughs at a' that.

27 *aboon:* above
28 *mauna fa' that:* must not try that
36 *bear the gree:* have the first place

✦ *Activities*

1 The speaker repeatedly uses *we*. Pick out all the expressions which refer to this group of people and outline their way of life, their character and their opinions. Contrast them with the other group in the poem.

2 Pick out the other phrases which develop the idea expressed in:
   The rank is but the guinea's stamp.
   Contrast this with the idea expressed in *the gowd* and the phrases which develop it.
   Discuss the principle on which Burns is distinguishing between people.

3 What is the meaning and the tone of the repeated phrase *For a' that and a' that*? How does it set the tone of the whole poem?

4 Arrange a choral reading of this poem, using contrasting voices and various groupings of voices to bring out its rhythm and its high points.

5 You are a member of The Friends of the People, a 'seditious' democratic group in Glasgow in the 1790s. Pick out some good slogans from this poem and work them into a handbill for secret distribution.

A prince can mak' a belted knight,   25
    A marquis, duke, and a' that;
But an honest man's aboon his might,
    Gude faith, he mauna fa' that!
For a' that, and a' that,
    Their dignities, and a' that;   30
The pith o' sense, and pride o' worth,
    Are higher rank than a' that.

Then let us pray that come it may,
    As come it will for a' that,
That sense and worth, o'er a' the earth,   35
    May bear the gree, and a' that:
For a' that, and a' that,
    It's comin' yet for a' that,
That man to man, the warld o'er,
    Shall brothers be for a' that!   40

Notes on 'O, wert thou in the cauld blast'

Background

Burns was in his last illness and lay dying. He was nursed by
18-year-old Jessie Lewars, a sister of one of his fellow excisemen.
He heard her singing an old tune and wrote her new words for it.
He had already written words to many old tunes for the great song
collections to which he had contributed. This was his last song but
one.

Verse form

Tetrameter lines grouped in eight-line stanzas to match the length
of the tune.

---

   2 *lea:*   meadow
   3 *plaidie:*   woollen cloak
       airt: direction
   7 *bield:*   shelter
9–11 These lines describe a very Scottish type of
       inhospitable and harsh landscape. *The desert* is
       uninhabited land.
  16 *wad:*   would

✦ *Activities*

1 Describe the changing emotions conveyed in this poem.

2 Some of the images used in this poem are close to those in
'Yestreen I had a pint o' wine' (page 91). Discuss how it is
possible that the same ideas can be used to different effect in
the two poems.

3 Can you do what Burns did here? Take a tune you know and
love, preferably one without words, and invent a stanza or two
which is in harmony with its mood.

O, wert thou in the cauld blast

TUNE: *Lenox love to Blantyre*

O, wert thou in the cauld blast
   On yonder lea, on yonder lea,
My plaidie to the angry airt,
   I'd shelter thee, I'd shelter thee.
Or did Misfortune's bitter storms   5
   Around thee blaw, around thee blaw,
Thy bield should be my bosom,
   To share it a', to share it a'.

Or were I in the wildest waste,
   Sae black and bare, sae black and bare,   10
The desert were a Paradise,
   If thou wert there, if thou wert there.
Or were I monarch of the globe,
   Wi' thee to reign, wi' thee to reign,
The brightest jewel in my crown   15
   Wad be my queen, wad be my queen.

AN APPENDIX OF POEMS WHICH INFLUENCED BURNS

✦

A predecessor of 'Holy Willie's Prayer'

Notes on 'The Last Speech of a Wretched Miser'

Allan Ramsay's poetry (1684–1758) was well known to Burns (see pages 162 and 174). We know from his letters that he read Ramsay's works in his youth and it seems possible that the following poem influenced him. There were, however, other dramatic monologues in Scottish and English literature before Burns.

---

 1 *Dool*:   pain
 2 *siller*:   money
 5 *Gowd*:   gold
   Bands: bonds
   alakanie: alas
 9 *Caff*:   chaff
14 *Fowk*:   folk
15 *sell*:   self
17 *Pouch*:   pocket
   Ingan: onion
18 *Wame*:   stomach

Allan Ramsay

extracts from
The Last Speech of a Wretched Miser

O Dool! and am I forc'd to die,
And nae mair my dear siller see,
That glanc'd sae sweetly in my Eye!
    It breaks my Heart;
My Gowd! my Bands! alakanie!   5
     That we shou'd part.

For you I labour'd Night and Day,
For you I did my Friends betray,
For you on stinking Caff I lay,
    And Blankets thin;   10
And for your Sake fed mony a Flea
     Upon my skin.

     * * * * * * *

Altho' my Annual rents cou'd feed
Thrice forty Fowk that stood in Need,
I grudg'd my sell my daily Bread: 15
    And if frae hame,
My Pouch produc'd an Ingan Head,
     To please my Wame.

     * * * * * * *

19 *Gear*:   property
21 *Virginia*:   the colony of Virginia on the east coast of the USA
   sald: sold as a slave
23 *gawn I kenna whither*:   going I know not where
25 *earns*:   worries about
27 *Sic*:   such
   laigh: low
29 *Rotle*:   death rattle
30 *maun*:   must
39 *Dub-water*:   ditchwater
   skink: pour out
41 *gar*:   make
   dwine: dwindle

O Gear! I held ye lang thegither;
For you I starved my good auld Mither,   20
And to *Virginia* sald my Brither,
                And crush'd my Wife:
But now I'm gawn I kenna whither,
                To leave my Life.

My Life! my God! my Spirit earns,   25
Not on my Kindred, Wife or Bairns,
Sic are but very laigh Concerns,
                Compared with thee!
When now this mortal Rotle warns
                Me I maun die.   30

It to my Heart gaes like a gun,
To see my Kin and graceless Son,
Like Rooks already are begun
                To thumb my Gear,
And Cash that has not seen the Sun   35
                This fifty Year.

Oh, oh! that spendthrift Son of mine,
Wha can on roasted Moorfowl dine,
And like Dub-water skink the Wine,
                And dance and sing;   40
He'll soon gar my dear Darlings dwine
                Down to nathing.

45 *fang*:   seize
47 *Woodies*:   gallows
48 *breaking*:   burgling
51 *play'd a pew*:   drew a breath
52 *Rair*:   roar
54 *It maksna where*:   It doesn't matter where.

To that same Place, where e'er I gang,
O cou'd I bear my Wealth alang!
Nae Heir shou'd e'er a Farthing fang, 45
        That thus carouses.
Tho' they shou'd a' on Woodies hang,
        For breaking Houses.

Perdition! Sathan! is that you!
I sink! — am dizzy! — Candle blue. 50
Wi' that he never mair play'd a pew,
        But with a Rair,
Away his wretched Spirit flew,
        It maksna where.

Influences on 'The Cotter's Saturday Night'

James Thomson

James Thomson (1700–1748) was a Scot who surrendered entirely to English influence and became a major landscape poet. Note the archaic language derived from the poet Edmund Spenser (*The Faerie Queene*, 1596), which Burns echoes. Thomson and Burns both use the Spenserian stanza (see page 181).

James Thomson

extracts from *The Castle of Indolence* (1748)

In lowly dale, fast by a river's side,
   With woody hill o'er hill encompass'd round,
A most enchanting Wizard did abide,
   Than whom a fiend more fell is no where found.
    It was, I ween, a lovely spot of ground;   5
And there a season atween June and May,
   Half prankt with spring, with summer half imbrown'd,
A listless climate made, where, sooth to say,
No living wight could work, ne cared even for play.

           * * * * * *

Joined to the prattle of the purling rills,   10
   Were heard the lowing herds along the vale,
And flocks loud-bleating from the distant hills,
   And vacant shepherds piping in the dale:
    And now and then sweet Philomel would wail,
Or stock-doves 'plain amid the forest deep,
   That drowsy rustled to the sighing gale;   15
And still a coil the grasshopper did keep:
Yet all these sounds yblent inclined all to sleep.

James Beattie
James Beattie (1735–1803) was another Scottish poet, an older
contemporary of Burns. (See also page 162.) Here are two
high-sounding stanzas from *The Minstrel*, which was much
admired by Burns. It too is in Spenserian stanza with the
characteristic archaic vocabulary.

James Beattie

extracts from *The Minstrel* (1771)

Hence! ye, who snare and stupify the mind,
    Sophists! of beauty, virtue, joy, the bane!
Greedy and fell, though impotent and blind,
    Who spread your filthy nets in Truth's fair fane,
    And ever ply your venom'd fangs amain!   5
Hence to dark Error's den, whose rankling slime
    First gave you form! Hence! lest the Muse should deign
(Though loth on theme so mean to waste a rhyme),
With vengeance to pursue your sacrilegious crime.

*   *   *   *   *   *

But who the melodies of morn can tell?   10
    The wild brook babbling down the mountain side;
The lowing herd; the sheepfold's simple bell;
    The pipe of early shepherd dim descried
    In the lone valley; echoing far and wide
The clamorous horn along the cliffs above;   15
    The hollow murmur of the ocean-tide;
The hum of bees, the linnet's lay of love,
And the full choir that wakes the universal grove.

Notes on 'The Farmer's Ingle'

Robert Fergusson (1750–1774) was an Edinburgh poet whose work showed Burns that it was possible to write poetry in Scots (see pages 162 and 174). 'The Farmer's Ingle' was a strong influence on 'The Cotter's Saturday Night'. It is a richly dialectal and realistic picture of a Scottish peasant's home. Fergusson's use of a modified Spenserian stanza (see page 181) clearly influenced Burns's choice of verse form for this subject.

The epigraph at the head of the poem translates as: 'If it's going to be cold, it's best to have plenty of food, drink and jollity around the fire.' (Virgil, Bucolics)

1 *glowmin*:   twilight
2 *caws*:   drives
   owsen: oxen
3 *sair dung*:   sorely beaten
   steeks: closes
4 *histy*:   fast working
   dightin':   winnowing corn
5 *bangs fu' leal*:   attacks very thoroughly
6 *gars*:   makes
7 *dowie*:   downcast
10 *winnow't*:   dried by the wind
11 *divets*:   turfs
   theekit: thatched
13 *smeek*:   smoke
   lift: sky
15 *hallan*:   partition in a cottage
16 *ilka turn is handled to his mind*:   each job is done as he wishes
18 *looes*:   loves

Robert Fergusson

extracts from *The Farmer's Ingle* (1772)

Et multo in primis hilarans convivia Baccho,
Ante focum, si frigus erit.

Virgil, Bucolics

I

Whan glowmin grey out owre the welkin keeks;
    Whan Bawtie caws his owsen to the byre;
Whan Thrasher John, sair dung, his barn-door steeks,
    And histy lasses at the dightin' tire;
What bangs fu' leal the e'ening's comin' cauld,   5
    And gars snaw-tappit Winter freeze in vain;
Gars dowie mortals look baith blyth and bauld,
     Nor fley'd wi' a' the poortith o' the plain;
     Begin, my Muse! and chaunt in hamely strain.

II

Frae the big stack, weel winnow't on the hill,   10
    Wi' divets theekit frae the weet and drift,
Sods, peats, and heathery turfs the chimley fill,
    And gar their thick'ning smeek salute the lift.
The gudeman, new come hame, is blythe to find,
    Whan he out owre the hallan flings his een,   15
That ilka turn is handled to his mind,
     That a' his housie looks sae cosh and clean;
     For cleanly house looes he, though e'er sae mean.

19 *sickan*:   such
21 *weirlike*:   warlike
22 *bruilzies*:   battles
23 *gardies*:   arms
25 *yird*:   earth
26 *Gar'd*:   made
    bang: beat
27 *doughtna*:   could not
28 *couthy cracks*:   friendly chats
29 *bicker*:   cup
    gars: makes
    gash: chat
31 *mailen's*:   farm's
    hash: destroy
32 *eke*:   also
35 *cutty-stool*:   stool of repentence (see also page 16)
36 *scauld*:   scolding
    Mess John: priest
    bide: suffer

* * * * * *

V

On sickan food has mony a doughty deed
 By Caledonia's ancestors been done;   20
By this did mony a wight fu' weirlike bleed
 In bruilzies frae the dawn to set o' sun.
'Twas this that brac'd their gardies stiff and strang;
 That bent the deadly yew in ancient days;
Laid Denmark's daring sons on yird alang;   25
 Gar'd Scottish thristles bang the Roman bays;
 For near our crest their heads they doughtna raise.

VI

The couthy cracks begin whan supper's owre;
 The cheering bicker gars them glibly gash
O' Simmer's showery blinks, and Winters sour, 30
 Whase floods did erst their mailen's produce hash.
'Bout kirk and market eke their tales gae on;
 How Jock woo'd Jenny here to be his bride;
And there, how Marion, for a bastard son,
 Upo' the cutty-stool was forc'd to ride;   35
 The waefu' scauld o' our Mess John to bide.

37 *fient*:   devil
39 *maun*:   must
   fastin mou':   fasting mouth
40 *greet*:   weep
   mak an unco mane: make a great outcry
41 *rangles*:   clusters
   ingle's low: fire's flame
43 *loupin*:   leaping
   wirrikow: hobgoblin
44 *win*:   dwell
45 *touzles a' their tap*:   makes their hair stand on end
47 *fells*:   supplies
48 *sock and cou'ter*:   ploughshare
   glybe: field
49 *bauks*:   strips
51 *decreed*:   protected
52 *bien*:   prosperous
53 *ails*:   illnesses
   poortith: poverty

VII

The fient a cheep's amang the bairnies now;
 For a' their anger's wi' their hunger gane;
Ay maun the childer, wi' a fastin mou',
 Grumble, and greet, and mak an unco mane. 40
In rangles round before the ingle's low,
 Frae gudame's mouth auld-warld tales they hear,
O' warlocks loupin round the wirrikow;
  O' ghaists that win in glen and kirkyard drear,
  Whilk touzles a' their tap, and gars them shake wi' fear! 45

* * * * * *

XIII

Peace to the husbandman and a' his tribe,
 Whase care fells a' our wants frae year to year!
Lang may his sock and cou'ter turn the glybe,
 And bauks o' corn bend down wi' laded ear!
May Scotia's simmers ay look gay and green; 50
 Her yellow har'sts frae scowry blasts decreed!
May a' her tenants sit fu' snug and bien,
  Frae the hard grip o' ails and poortith freed;
  And a lang lasting train o' peacefu' hours succeed!

Thomas Gray

extracts from
Elegy Written in a Country Church-yard
(1750)

The Curfew tolls the knell of parting day,
    The lowing herd wind slowly o'er the lea,
The ploughman homeward plods his weary way,
    And leaves the world to darkness, and to me.

Now fades the glimmering landscape on the sight,   5
    And all the air a solemn stillness holds,
Save where the beetle wheels his droning flight,
    And drowsy tinklings lull the distant folds.

       * * * * * *

Beneath those rugged elms, that yew-tree's shade,
    Where heaves the turf in many a mould'ring heap,   10
Each in his narrow cell for ever laid,
    The rude Forefathers of the hamlet sleep.

       * * * * * *

For them no more the blazing hearth shall burn,
    Or busy housewife ply her evening care:
No children run to lisp their sire's return,   15
    Or climb his knees the envied kiss to share.

       * * * * * *

Let not Ambition mock their useful toil,
    Their homely joys, and destiny obscure;
Nor Grandeur hear with a disdainful smile,
    The short and simple annals of the Poor.   20

The boast of heraldry, the pomp of pow'r,
    And all that beauty, all that wealth e'er gave,
Awaits alike th' inevitable hour:–
    The paths of glory lead but to the grave.

Nor you, ye Proud, impute to these the fault,   25
    If Mem'ry o'er their Tomb no Trophies raise,
Where through the long-drawn aisle and fretted vault
    The pealing anthem swells the note of praise.

Can storied urn or animated bust
    Back to its mansion call the fleeting breath?   30
Can Honour's voice provoke the silent dust,
    Or Flatt'ry soothe the dull cold ear of Death?

                  * * * * * *

Far from the madding crowd's ignoble strife,
    Their sober wishes never learn'd to stray;
Along the cool sequester'd vale of life   35
    They kept the noiseless tenor of their way.

Influences on 'The Twa Dogs'

Notes on 'Mutual Complaint of Plainstanes and Causey in their Mother-Tongue'

The plainstanes are the flagstones of the pavement in Edinburgh and the causey is the cobbled roadway. The pavement is given the more genteel and delicate character, whereas the roadway is more stoutly and coarsely made. The poem is a dialogue between these two in which they both complain about overwork. Plainstanes thinks that only refined people should be allowed on the pavement.

---

1 *thir*: these
2 *forfoughen*: overworked
   ear': early
4 *thrawart*: unfortunate
   bure: bore
6 *ilk ane*: each one
   stent: task
7 *to flyte I'se e'en be bauld*: to scold I shall even be bold
8 *sic*: such
   thrall'd: enslaved
9 *haps it*: comes it about
10 *Hair-kaimers, crieshy gizy-makers*: hair combers, greasy wig-makers
13 *crackit*: spoken   *aft hauds*: often holds
14 *fouk mak maist ado*: folk make the biggest fuss
15 *Weel ken ye, though ye doughtna tell*: Well you know, though you can't bring yourself to admit
16 *the sairest kane*: the heaviest penalty
17 *Owre*: over
18 *birr*: bruise
19 *muckle*: big
20 *rug*: tug   *saul*: soul

Robert Fergusson

extracts from
Mutual Complaint of Plainstanes and Causey in their Mother-Tongue (1774)

* * * * * *

Plainstanes

My friend! thir hunder years and mair,
We've been forfoughen late and ear',
In sunshine and in weety weather,
Our thrawart lot we bure thegither.
I never growl'd, but was content   5
Whan ilk ane had an equal stent;
But now to flyte I'se e'en be bauld,
Whan I'm wi' sic a grievance thrall'd.
How haps it, say, that mealy bakers,
Hair-kaimers, crieshy gizy-makers,   10
Shou'd a' get leave to waste their powders
Upon my beaux' and ladies' shoulders?

* * * * * *

Causey

Weel crackit, friend! – It aft hauds true,
Wi' naething fouk mak maist ado.
Weel ken ye, though ye doughtna tell,   15
I pay the sairest kane mysel:
Owre me, ilk day, big waggons rumble,
And a' my fabric birze and jumble.
Owre me the muckle horses gallop,
Eneugh to rug my very saul up.   20

* * * * * *

Notes on 'The Borrowstoun Mous and the Landwart Mous'

This version of 'The Borrowstoun Mous' was known to Burns in *The Ever Green*, edited by Allan Ramsay, 1724 (see page 162). Ramsay has altered it greatly from Henryson's original, and most readers would agree that it is an inferior poem; but nonetheless it transmitted to Burns something valuable of the literary tradition of Scots poetry. The original, and much superior, poem is in Henryson's 'Morall Fabillis of Esope the Phrygian' and was originally called 'The Taill of the Uponlandis Mous and the Burges Mous'. (See page 161.) It was written about 1480 and stands in the long tradition of poems about animals with human characteristics which goes back to the ancient Greeks.

---

1 *Cheir*: joy
  sene: seen
2 *thir*: these
3 *Quhilk*: which
4 *quhyls*: sometimes
  leuch: laughed
  grat: wept
5 *plet*: enfolded
6 *fure*: travelled
  sobirt: calm
  Meid: mood
7 *Syne*: then
  Chalmer: room
  yeid: went
8 *hard*: heard   *semple Wane*: simple dwelling
9 *Fog*: foliage   *fecklesly*: roughly
10 *silly Sheil*: simple shelter   *Eard*: earth
11 *hie*: high   *braid*: broad
12 *bot mair abaid*: without more delay
13 *birnand*: burning
14 *Pykers*: pilferers

Robert Henryson

extracts from
The Borrowstoun Mous
and the Landwart Mous
(much altered by Allan Ramsay)

The town mouse has set out to visit her sister, the country
mouse. The country mouse has come to meet her.

* * * * * *

Thair hearty Cheir was plesand to be sene,
    Quhen thir twa Sisters kind with Blythness met,
Quhilk aften Syss was shawin them twa betwein;
    For quhyls they leuch, and quhyls for Joy they grat,
    Quhyls sweitly kist, and quhyls in Arms they plet: 5
And thus they fure, till sobirt was thair Meid,
Syne Fute for Fute they to thair Chalmer yeid.

As I hard say, it was a semple Wane
    Of Fog and Fern, full fecklesly was maid,
A silly Sheil, under a Eard-fast Stane,   10
    Of quhilk the Entrie was not hie nor braid;
    Into the same they went bot mair abaid,
Withouten Fyre or Candle birnand bricht,
For commonly sic Pykers luves not Licht.

15 *lugit*:   lodged
    thir: these
    silly: harmless
16 *Butrie*:   larder
    hyed: went
18 *sic plain Cheir*:   such plain food
19 *dynk*:   finely dressed
21 *quod scho*:   said she
    Mess: food
22 *be my Saul*:   by my soul
29 *thyne*:   thence
    on till: unto
    Wane: dwelling
31 *God-speid*:   God's blessing
    Herboury: shelter
32 *Spence*:   larder
    Vittell: food
33 *Skelfs*:   shelves
    hie: high
35 *Pokks*:   bags
    Grots: corn

Quhen thus wer lugit thir twa silly Myce, 15
    The yungest Sister to her Butrie hyed,
And brocht furth Nuts and Peis insteid of Spyce,
    And sic plain Cheir as scho had her besyde:
    The Burges Mous sae dynk and full of Pryde,
Sayd, Sister myne, Is this your daylie Fude? 20
Quhy not, quod scho, think ye this Mess not gude?

Na, be my Saul, methink it but a Scorn;
    Madame, quod scho, ye be the mair to blame:
My Moder said, aftir that we wer born,
    That ye and I lay baith within her Wame; 25
    I keip the richt auld Custom of my Dame
And of my Syre, – livand in Povertie,
For Lands and Rents nane is our Propertie.

* * * * * *

The town mouse takes her sister to her home in a large
town house.

Not far frae thyne, on till a worthy Wane,
    This Burges brocht them sune quhair they sould be, 30
Without God-speid, – thair Herboury was tane
    Intill a Spence, wher Vittell was Plenty,
    Baith Cheis and Butter on lang Skelfs richt hie,
With Fish and Flesh enough baith fresh and salt,
And Pokks full of Grots, Barlie, Meil and Malt. 35

37 *wush*:   washed
39 *Telyies grit*:   thick slices
40 *Erles Fair*:   earl's food
    can: did
43 *quhyle*:   until
    micht: could manage
48 *Spens*:   butler
    Keis: keys
49 *Apent*:   opened
    fand: found
51 *quha micht the foremost win*:   whoever could gain the
    foremost place
54 *silly*:   poor
55 *disalait*:   desolate
    will of all gude reid: lacking all good advice

Quhen afterwart they wer disposd to dyne,
    Withouten Grace they wush and went to meit,
On every Dish that Cuikmen can divyne,
    Muttone and Beif cut out in Telyies grit,
    Ane Erles Fair thus can they counterfitt,   40
Exept ane Thing, — they drank the Watter cleir
Insteid of Wyne, but yit they made gude Cheir.

* * * * * *

Thus made they mirry, quhyle they micht nae mair,
    And hail *Yule!* hail! they all cryt up on hie;
But after Joy ther aftentymes comes Cair,   45
    And Trouble after grit Prosperitie:
    Thus as they sat in all thair Jolitie,
The Spens came on them with Keis in his Hand,
Apent the Dore, and them at Dinner fand.

They tarriet not to wash, ye may suppose,   50
    But aff they ran, quha micht the foremost win;
The Burges had a Hole, and in scho gaes,
    Her Sister had nae Place to hyde her in,
    To see that silly Mous it was grit Sin,
Sae disalait and will of all gude reid,   55
For very Feir scho fell in Swoun, neir deid.

* * * * * *

Influences on 'Address to the Deil'

John Milton

extracts from *Paradise Lost* (1667)

Milton told how the Devil, known as Satan, had been at first an angel in Heaven with God and all the other angels. He then led a rebellion against God. He and his supporters were defeated and fell from Heaven. They became the devils of Hell.

A. In the extract from which Burns quoted the epigraph to 'Address to the Deil', Beelzebub, a fallen angel, addresses Satan.

'O Prince, O Chief of many thronèd Powers
That led the embattled Seraphim to war
Under thy conduct, and, in dreadful deeds
Fearless, endangered Heaven's perpetual King,
And put to proof his high supremacy,   5
Whether upheld by strength, or chance, or fate,
Too well I see and rue the dire event
That, with sad overthrow and foul defeat,
Hath lost us Heaven, and all this mighty host
In horrible destruction laid thus low,   10
As far as God's and Heavenly Essences
Can perish: for the mind and spirit remains
Invincible, and vigour soon returns,
Though all our glory extinct, and happy state
Here swallowed up in endless misery.   15
                          Book One, lines 128–142

B. The following passage is part of Milton's description of Adam and Eve in the Garden of Eden.

Two of far nobler shape, erect and tall,
God-like erect, with native honour clad
In naked majesty, seemed lords of all,
And worthy seemed; for in their looks divine
The image of their glorious Maker shone,   5
Truth, wisdom, sanctitude severe and pure —
Severe, but in true filial freedom placed,
Whence true authority in men: though both
Not equal, as their sex not equal seemed;
For contemplation he and valour formed,   10
For softness she and sweet attractive grace;
He for God only, she for God in him.

* * * * * *

So hand in hand they passed, the loveliest pair
That ever since in love's embraces met —
Adam the goodliest man of men since born   15
His sons; the fairest of her daughters Eve.
Under a tuft of shade that on a green
Stood whispering soft, by a fresh fountain-side,
They sat them down ...
Nor gentle purpose, nor endearing smiles   20
Wanted, nor youthful dalliance, as beseems
Fair couple linked in happy nuptial league,
Alone as they.
                Book Four, lines 288–299 and 321–340

Predecessors of 'Auld lang syne'

Burns seems to have been reworking an old folksong. In a letter he praised the 'heaven-inspired poet who composed this glorious fragment'.

In 1720, Allan Ramsay had published his own words to the tune of a street song:

Should auld acquaintance be forgot
Tho they return with scars?

John Skinner wrote 'The Old Minister's Song':

Should auld acquaintance be forgot,
    Or friendship e'er grow cauld?
Should we nae tighter draw the knot
    Ae as we're growing auld?

How comes it, then, my worthy friend,
    Wha used to be sae kin',
We dinna for ilk ither speir
    As we did lang syne?

Francis Sempill also wrote a poem called 'Auld lang syne'.

The origins of 'Tam o' Shanter'

Here is Burns's original English prose version of the tale, set out in a letter to Captain Grose in June 1790:

On a market-day, in the town of Ayr, a farmer from Carrick, and consequently whose way lay by the very gate of Aloway [sic] kirk-yard, in order to cross the river Doon, at the old bridge, which is about two or three hundred yards further on than the said gate, had been detained by his business 'till by the time he reached Aloway it was the wizard hour, between night and morning.

Though he was terrified with a blaze streaming from the kirk, yet as it is a well known fact, that to turn back on these occasions is running by far the greatest risk of mischief, he prudently advanced on his road. When he had reached the gate of the kirk-yard, he was surprised and entertained, through the ribs and arches of an old gothic window which still faces the highway, to see a dance of witches merrily footing it round their old sooty blackguard master, who was keeping them alive with the powers of his bagpipe. The farmer stopping his horse to observe them a little, could plainly desern [sic] the faces of many old women of his acquaintance and neighbourhood. How the gentleman was dressed, tradition does not say; but the ladies were all in their smocks; and one of them happening unluckily to have a smock which was considerably too short to answer all the purpose of that piece of dress, our farmer was so tickled that he involuntarily burst out, with a loud laugh, 'Weel luppen, Maggy wi' the short sark!' and recollecting himself, instantly spurred his horse to the top of his speed. I need not mention the universally known fact, that no diabolical power can pursue you beyond the middle of a running stream. Lucky it was for the poor farmer that the river Doon was so near, for notwithstanding the speed of his horse, which was a good one, against he reached the middle of the arch of the bridge and consequently the middle of the stream, the pursuing, vengeful hags were so close at his heels, that one of them actually sprung [sic] to seize him: but it was too late;

nothing was on her side of the stream but the horse's tail, which immediately gave way to her infernal grip, as if blasted by a stroke of lightning; but the farmer was beyond her reach. However, the unsightly, tailless condition of the vigorous steed was to the last hours of the noble creature's life, an awful warning to the Carrick farmers, not to stay too late in Ayr markets.

Homer

The Iliad
extracts from Pope's translation (1715–1720)

This translation of Homer was very widely read and influential in the 18th century. It and Milton's *Paradise Lost* set the standard for epic style in English poetry. Here is a typical example of Pope's style from *The Iliad*, Book VIII. Trojan troops are eagerly awaiting dawn and a battle which they expect to win. Note the dignified language and the long epic simile, lines 3–16.

The troops exulting sat in order round,
And beaming Fires illumined all the Ground.
As when the Moon, refulgent Lamp of Night!
O'er Heaven's clear Azure spreads her sacred Light,
When not a Breath disturbs the deep Serene;   5
And not a Cloud o'ercasts the solemn Scene;
Around her Throne the vivid Planets roll,
And Stars unnumbered gild the glowing Pole,
O'er the dark Trees a yellower Verdure shed,
And tip with Silver every Mountain's Head;   10
Then shine the Vales, the Rocks in Prospect rise,
A Flood of Glory bursts from all the Skies:
The conscious Swains, rejoicing in the Sight,
Eye the blue Vault, and bless the useful Light.
So many flames before proud *Ilion* blaze,   15
And lighten glimmering *Xanthus* with their Rays.
The long Reflections of the distant Fires

Gleam on the Walls, and tremble on the Spires.
A thousand Piles the dusky Horrors gild,
And shoot a shady Lustre o'er the Field.   20
Full fifty Guards each flaming Pile attend,
Whose umbered Arms, by fits, thick Flashes send.
Loud neigh the Coursers o'er their Heaps of Corn,
And ardent Warriors wait the rising Morn.

An older version of 'John Anderson my Jo'

from *The Merry Muses of Caledonia*

John Anderson, my jo, John,
    When first that ye began,
Ye had as good a tail-tree,
    As any ither man;
But now its waxen wan, John,   5
    And wrinkles to and fro;
I've twa gae-ups for ae gae-down,
    John Anderson, my jo.

I'm backit like a salmon,
    I'm breastit like a swan;   10
My wame it is a down-cod,
    My middle ye may span:
Frae my tap-knot to my tae, John,
    I'm like the new-fa'n snow;
And it's a' for your convenience,   15
    John Anderson, my jo.

Predecessors of 'A red red Rose'

O, she's like a new-strung instrument
That's newly put in tune.
            (Broadside ballad in the Roxburghe Collection)

Altho' I go ten thousand miles
I'll come again to thee, dear love.

The Day shall turn to night, dear love,
And the Rocks melt with the Sun,
Before that I prove false to thee.
                              (Song)

Fare you well, my own true love,
And fare you well for a while,
And I will be sure to return back again,
If I go ten thousand mile.
                  ('The True Lover's Farewell')

RESOURCE NOTES

Who has written these poems and why?

Robert Burns was the eldest son of a smallholder and market gardener near the town of Ayr in south-west Scotland. His father soon moved to the tenancy of a nearby small farm. Burns had short periods of schooling at ages 6 to 9 and again at ages 10 and 14. By his early teens he was his father's main labourer on a small farm of very poor soil with no mechanical equipment – a heavy physical burden which is thought to have so strained his heart that it contributed to his early death. In his teens he studied French and surveying for a few weeks in each of two summers. From the age of 23 or 24, when he read the Scots poems of Allan Ramsay (1684–1758) and Robert Fergusson (1750–1774), he began to think of himself as a poet and began a Commonplace Book containing notes of his thoughts and poetical attempts.

Neither father nor son was successful at farming. As their father sank towards financial ruin and death, Robert and his younger brother Gilbert took on a new farm tenancy at Mossgiel in a neighbouring district of Ayrshire. Burns became head of the family, consisting of his mother and six brothers and sisters. This was the period of his most earnest farming and intense poetry writing. His poems were admired locally but he was also gaining a reputation as a womaniser.

He seems to have started his affair with Jean Armour, the daughter of a local builder, in 1785, when he was 26. The truth of the succeeding events is obscure. At that time in Scotland it was possible to contract a legal marriage by declaration and consummation. Burns seems to have considered himself married to Jean but her parents forced her to disown him. He began an affair with Mary Campbell (better known as Highland Mary) and may have promised to marry her. He seems to have feared at one point in 1786 that he might be arrested for bigamy. He planned to emigrate to Jamaica (probably with Mary) but was finally dissuaded by the success of his first publication, the Kilmarnock edition, and the prospect of fame in Edinburgh.

In those days a poet without private means had to secure the support of someone rich and influential in order to become widely known. The next two years were occupied in cultivating potential patrons, several sight-seeing (and song collecting) trips around Scotland and visits to Edinburgh and back to Mossgiel. Meanwhile his fame spread throughout the United Kingdoms.

Burns might have expected to obtain a sinecure (a light job with a good salary) from some aristocratic admirer but the outcome was merely the tenancy of another rather poor farm (Ellisland, near Dumfries) and a training to be an exciseman (a customs officer). At this time he finally established his marriage to Jean, who had by now borne him two sets of twins. From now on, his main poetic activity was the collecting and writing of songs. In this last phase of his life he was the family man, the famous poet, the regular churchgoer and the citizen of Dumfries, where he set up house in 1791 as a full-time exciseman. This did not prevent him from having several affairs with local girls or from getting into serious trouble with the authorities for his anti-government remarks.

Throughout his life he seduced a succession of women, mostly his social inferiors, young, ill-educated and easily impressed. He had less success with women his intellectual equals. About his undoubted heavy drinking there are several opinions. His immense industry at all periods of his life refutes the old assertion that he was a habitual drunkard, and modern medical opinion concludes that his frequent bouts of severe illness and his death were caused by rheumatic fever, not alcoholism.

In contrast to the accusations of sedition levelled against him in 1792, he was given a civic and military funeral procession in Dumfries, complete with the Provost and Town Council, the local Masonic lodge, a regimental band, and volleys fired over the open grave by the militia unit that he had helped to form.

Dates	Burns's poems against the background of the times
1688–89	'The Glorious Revolution': presbyterianism is finally established as Scotland's state church.
1707	The Union of the Parliaments: the end of Scotland as an independent nation.
1715	The first Jacobite Rebellion fails to restore the Stuart dynasty.
1722	The last execution for witchcraft in Scotland.
1724	Allan Ramsay's poetry collections published.
1745–46	The second Jacobite Rebellion (Bonnie Prince Charlie). The Highlands subdued by Government troops.
1759	Robert Burns born.
1771–74	Robert Fergusson's poems appear in Edinburgh.
1776	American Declaration of Independence.
1783	End of the American War of Independence.
1784–85	'Holy Willie's Prayer' and 'To a Louse' written.
1785	May: 'To William Simpson, Ochiltree' and 'A Poet's Welcome to his love-begotten Daughter' written.
	November: 'To a Mouse' written; 'Love and Liberty' probably written.
1785–86	'The Cotter's Saturday Night', 'The Twa Dogs' and 'Address to the Deil' written.
1786	July: The Kilmarnock Edition published, omitting 'Holy Willie's Prayer', 'A Poet's Welcome' and 'Love and Liberty'.
	November: first visit to Edinburgh.
1787	April: First Edinburgh Edition published. First meeting with James Johnson the music publisher: Burns begins folksong collecting.
1788	'Auld lang syne' written; 'I hae a wife o' my ain' probably written.

1789	The fall of the Bastille. Declaration of the Rights of Man by French Constituent Assembly.
1790	'Tam o' Shanter' and 'Yestreen I had a pint o' wine' written. *The Scots Musical Museum*, volume 3, published by Johnson, containing 'John Anderson my Jo'.
1791	'Ae fond kiss' written.
1792	*Rights of Man* by Thomas Paine published (see page 166). 'Such a parcel of rogues in a nation' written. *The Scots Musical Museum*, volume 4, published, containing 'Ae fond kiss' and 'Such a parcel'. Burns starts work for Thomson's *Select Collection of Original Scottish Airs*.
	September: September Massacres in Paris.
1793	January: Execution of King and Queen of France.
	February: Britain at war with France.
	Trial of the political reformer Thomas Muir in Edinburgh for sedition.
	Second Edinburgh Edition published containing 'Tam o' Shanter'. 'A red red Rose' written.
1794	'Scots, wha hae' published anonymously.
1795	'For a' that and a' that' written and published.
1796	'Oh wert thou in the cauld blast' written.
	July: Dies at Dumfries, probably of rheumatic fever.

The Scots language
The early stages

Scots is derived from the northernmost dialects of Anglo-Saxon, a Teutonic speech brought to Britain from northern Germany in the 5th century AD. Modern Standard English is derived from Anglo-Saxon dialects spoken in south-east England. Anglo-Saxons arrived in south-east Scotland about 600AD and their language evolved into Scots, influenced in the thirteenth century by incomers from north-east England bringing many Scandinavian features from their Viking past. Scots is totally distinct from Gaelic and steadily supplanted it until by the fourteenth century it had almost confined Gaelic to the Highlands.

From the fourteenth century, Scots was the dominant national language of an independent state and was used by all classes of society, from the king down, and for all purposes (other than those served by Latin). The classic period of late medieval Scots literature (Gavin Douglas, William Dunbar, Robert Henryson, David Lindsay) was from 1450 to 1550. From the sixteenth century onwards, Scots was increasingly influenced by its sister language, English. When James VI of Scotland became also James I of England in 1603, the centre of political power, patronage and fashion moved to London. English ways of speech and writing progressively claimed aspects of Scottish life. Through the 1611 translation of the Bible, English became increasingly the language of religion. Aspiring writers adopted the Anglicised language of their aristocratic patrons, who were aping the manners of the court in London. The union of the Scots Parliament with the English Parliament in 1707 marked the end of Scotland as a nation state and resulted in the writing of the laws of the United Kingdom in English and the advancement of the notion of Scotland as merely "North Britain". Yet even at that late date, the spoken language of the Scots Members of Parliament who went to Westminster was so distinct from that of their southern English colleagues that they could scarcely be understood.

The Scots language in the eighteenth century

Perhaps as a reaction to the final loss of national political identity with the Union of the Parliaments in 1707, a movement grew to rescue the traditions of national literature. Allan Ramsay (1684–1758) published *The Tea-Table Miscellany* and *The Ever Green* in 1724. The first was a collection of songs and ballads in Scots and the second was a collection of poems from the golden age of late medieval Scots writing, in 'modernised' versions. Both were immensely popular and influential. The process was continued by Robert Fergusson (1750–1774), the Edinburgh poet whose poems in Scots provided models for several of Burns's works.

On the other hand, some people in Scotland were enthusiastic about the creation of the United Kingdom by the Union of the Parliaments and sought to merge Scots cultural life into that of England. Thus, during the course of the eighteenth century many educated Scots sought to acquire a Southern English style of language. Some bought books such as *Scotticisms Arranged in Alphabetical Order, Designed to Correct Improprieties of Speech and Writing* (James Beattie, 1779). Some even took elocution lessons.

There were also the international advantages of using English. The mid-century group of Edinburgh intellectuals which included the philosopher David Hume (1711–1776) and the economist Adam Smith (1723–1790) were men of stature on the European stage and although they mostly spoke Scots, they saw English as the best medium through which to project Scotland as a centre of international culture. 'I am a citizen of the world,' wrote David Hume.

Thus Burns grew up at a time when Scots had been in steady decline for two centuries and had no dominant standard form. It had ceased to be the natural language of educated writing, but existed in a still vigorous tradition of poetry-writing and as a set of dialects spoken by rural people and by all ranks in informal conversation.

The language of Burns
Burns's education and upbringing made him familiar with English literature from his earliest years. He also learned enough French to read some literature in it and make frequent use of French phrases. Burns habitually wrote prose in English. In conversation with the intellectuals of Edinburgh, he spoke very good English.

However, the Scots influence was also strong on Burns in the language of his family and community and in particular through traditional songs and stories. He thus could move easily between the two languages, often mixing them, as many modern Scots do. As a result of his readings in Scots literature his local dialect was enriched by drawing on the older literary language of Scots.

Burns takes advantage of both Scots and English pronunciations to make rhymes. He borrowed his spelling system from Ramsay, who often used English spellings even when he clearly intended Scots sounds. In the bulk of his works Burns varies the degree of Scots or English vocabulary and pronunciation to suit his purpose. You have probably noticed how the richness of the dialect varies even from one part of a poem to another. Perhaps you can also detect how this relates to the topic and purpose of the poem. All told, he uses over 2000 exclusively Scots words; whereas most modern Scots speakers would use considerably less than 500. However, by his lifetime Scots had already fallen out of use for intellectual purposes and he could no longer find the range of abstract and speculative vocabulary which a fully functioning national language would have afforded him. Perhaps this brought out in him what the modern critic David Murison called the 'ability to fix in the vivid concrete terms of ordinary experience a universal truth', which has been the foundation of his popularity.

Pronunciation

Many Scots have lost the dialectal pronunciation to such an extent that, influenced by Burns's tendency to spell in anglicised conventions, they read the poetry in much too English a way to preserve its original flavour. It is to some extent a matter of taste how far Scots 'Scotticise' their reading of Burns's poetry. Non-Scottish readers should not feel that they are at much disadvantage.

The Burns Federation Song Book indicates, for example, that in 'Auld lang syne' we should pronounce 'Auld' as 'awl', 'forgot' as 'furgoat', 'brought' as 'broacht' and 'mind' to rhyme with 'syne'. 'Surely' is to sound as 'shairlay' and 'wander'd' as 'waunurt'.

In 'A red, red Rose', 'red' sounds as 'rid', 'so' as 'sae' and 'rocks' as 'roaks'.

In 'Scots, wha hae', 'hour' is to sound like 'oor', and 'lour' and 'power' to rhyme with it. The last line, 'Let us do or die', is to sound as 'Let us dae or dee'. Yet the same publication advises singers against the undoubtedly authentic pronunciations of 'thou' as 'thoo', 'joy' as 'jye', 'shall' as 'sall', and 'art' as 'airt'. So steer your own course.

The cultural background
Religion and superstition

The state church in Scotland, the Church of Scotland, was a presbyterian church totally distinct from the episcopalian Church of England, which was governed by a hierarchy of monarch, archbishop and bishops. It was organised in a hierarchy of assemblies, starting at local level with a gathering of Elders of the parish, the Kirk Session, presided over by the Minister; and progressing upwards through the district Presbytery and the regional Synod to the ultimate authority of the General Assembly. No one could escape its influence and authority in private and public life, although Scotland was noteworthy in the eighteenth and nineteenth centuries for the number of religious schisms it produced.

In Burns's time the Church of Scotland contained two tendencies: the more extreme Calvinist Auld Licht faction and the more progressive Moderates. The Auld Licht faction had narrower views on morals and on the fundamentalist interpretation of the Bible. They frowned on dancing, gambling, playing cards, working or travelling on a Sunday and going to the theatre. All forms of art, including literature, were distrusted and were to be severely controlled if tolerated at all. Burns leant towards the Moderate wing of the Church with its more liberal moral views and philosophic approach to theology. This aligned him with the better educated and therefore upper classes of the community, in spite of his identification in other respects with the labouring class in the countryside.

Burns's criticisms of narrow and dogmatic religion should not be taken as a rejection of all religion. He was a churchgoer to the last, though his kind of belief relied more on a philosophical conviction of the spiritual nature of mankind and the existence of a Supreme Being than on the teachings of revealed religion.

This links with his enthusiasm for Freemasonry. As well as acting as a friendly society for mutual support, Freemasonry in its Scottish form asserted a religious belief in a Supreme Being and the immortality of the soul. It stood for religious tolerance and universal brotherhood.

A third influence on Burns's beliefs was the tradition of folk tales and superstitions handed on to him by his mother's old relative and servant, Betty Davidson. It requires some understanding to grasp the tone of his references to witches. Burns makes fun of witches, which might lead us to suppose that people in his day regarded them much as we do now. But Burns's mockery is set against the superstition of the uneducated and the attitude of the extreme Calvinists, who emphasised the power of the Devil, the Enemy of Mankind, and still held witches to be his agents. The last execution for witchcraft in Scotland had occurred in 1722. The statutes against witchcraft were not repealed until 1735. When Burns was 14 years of age, the Secession Church re-affirmed its belief in witchcraft. You can work out the beliefs of the country people from his poetry, for Burns reproduces the standard ideas about witchcraft which had been widespread throughout Europe for centuries.

His wide reading and his adherence to the Moderates led him to mock the power attributed to the Devil and his servants the witches. However, it may be that Burns was able to make such vivid poetry out of witchcraft partly because he was not far removed from belief in it himself.

Radicalism

Burns lived through a time of great political ferment leading up to and during the French Revolution. The main intellectual movement in eighteenth-century Europe was the appeal to reason. This led political theorists to scrutinise established institutions. In England, one of the main propagandists for the new ideas was Thomas Paine (1737–1809). He emigrated to America, where he greatly influenced the writing of the American

Declaration of Independence (1776), with its total rejection of monarchy. Paine published *Rights of Man* in England in 1791–1792. Typical ideas from it are 'that all men are born equal'; 'Titles are but nick names'. Burns possessed a copy. During these years of political repression in Britain this was considered a sign of 'seditious' tendencies. However, when revolutionary France declared war on Britain, Burns became a patriot. As a customs official he had in any case to convince his superiors of his loyalty to the government or lose his job. In January 1795, he helped to found the Royal Dumfries Volunteers (an upper-class 'Territorial Army') to defend the country against invasion by France.

Back to nature

There was a growing fashion in Burns's time to regard the life of the countryside and the peasantry as more desirable than that of the town and the educated or fashionable citizens. The French philosopher Jean Jacques Rousseau (1712–1778) was a leading exponent of this view and spread the idea of the 'noble savage', the 'child of nature' who was somehow morally superior to the products of civilisation. One of the more extraordinary examples of this was the pretence of Queen Marie Antoinette of France (1755–1793) and her ladies to live the lives of shepherdesses in a purpose-built cottage in the grounds of Versailles Palace. Burns himself benefited from this fashion, for he was seized on by the intellectuals of Edinburgh society as in some respects the fulfilment of this ideal – the 'heaven inspired ploughman'. Burns at times represented himself in this guise for the sake of gaining favour with his public.

In the succeeding centuries the sentimental view of rural life accorded with the nostalgia felt by many Scottish town dwellers who had had a rural childhood, and this partly accounts for the popularity of Burns's poetry.

Life in the countryside

The social historians can give us some impression of what life was like for the common people in the countryside of eighteenth-century Scotland. Here is a short extract from *A History of the Scottish People 1560–1830* by T. C. Smout (Collins, 1977):

> A cottar's house, for instance, could be run up in a single day if the materials had been gathered beforehand. It was a stone-walled hut, with walls five foot high and twelve foot long on each side, an earth floor and a timber roof thatched with straw. Not all had chimneys – in many cottages the smoke rose from the hearth towards a hole left in the roof, or found its way out through the door or the unglazed window. The main piece of furniture in such a hovel was the box-bed, fully enclosed on all sides and accessible only by a sliding door in the front. – Otherwise there might be a couple of chests, two stools, a cooking pot, a wash tub, some wooden mugs and horn spoons to complete the inventory of a cottar's worldly goods. Two pecks of oatmeal weekly and adequate milk formed a major part of the hind's [farmworker's] wages, paid in kind, and their own kail-yard kept them in vegetables ... Their minute knowledge of the Bible [the cottars] also shared with the gudeman [the tenant farmer for whom they worked], together with the habit of regular household worship. There is something very astonishing in the prospect of a peasant society of very low average material standards in which everyone owns books or tracts, and is in the habit of discussing the scriptures with some knowledge and authority. ... [A cottar's house consisted of a but and a ben, an outer room and an inner room. In some cases] the peasant's cow lived in the ben and was only prevented from coming up to the fire-place by the box-bed that divided the house in two. One writer describes how his mother always knew it was time to put the porridge on the fire when she heard the family cow standing behind her pass water for the second time.

✦ *Activities*

1 Collect all the evidence you can from Burns's poems as to what the popular beliefs were about witches. Compare these with whatever information you can gather from reliable historical studies.

2 Look up the American Declaration of Independence, the Declaration of the Rights of Man and the ideas of Thomas Paine in a good encyclopaedia. You might get hold of the original wording of at least the first two documents. Make a wall display featuring memorable quotations from these sources. Search the poems to find similar ideas. Can you work quotations from Burns into your display and show links with the first set of quotations?

3 Find out more about Calvinist beliefs such as original sin, election and predestination. They have a logical coherence about them. Form two debating teams for and against their acceptance. (For this purpose everyone must assume the existence of God, Heaven and Hell.)

4 Scrutinise the language of the first four poems in this collection. List those words which are different from English only in their form and pronunciation. These are words in Scots which have a common ancestry with their English cousins but have evolved differently in the two languages. Try to write a series of rules for shaping English equivalents for Scots words. This may help you to work out the meaning of the Scots more quickly when reading the poems.

5 Find the writings of some other dialect authors in English: the poems of William Barnes (Dorset); the novels of John Steinbeck (USA), Emily Brontë (West Yorkshire), D. H. Lawrence (Nottinghamshire), Toni Morrison (Southern USA), Mildred D. Taylor (Southern USA), Lewis Grassic Gibbon (Scotland) or Sam Selvon (Trinidad); the short stories of Damon Runyon (New York). Show how far distant they are from Standard English as compared with Burns and what each writer's purpose was in using non-standard language.

6 Comment on the different ways in which Smout's description and Burns's 'The Cotter's Saturday Night' evoke the life of the Scottish peasantry in the eighteenth century. How would you describe the writer's purpose in each case?

———————————— ◆ ————————————

What type of texts are these poems?

Burns was influenced by several quite different traditions. In his own community and in his travels round Scotland he absorbed the Scots language and the rich traditions of Scottish folk song. In his formal education and his extensive reading he gained a close knowledge of some of the great works of Scottish and English literature. Through them he became aware of the established forms of European literature such as the ode and the epic. His poetry draws upon and transforms these established genres:

Satire

The purpose of satire is to attack aspects of human behaviour or of human nature. It can be delivered through almost any of the main forms of literature: novels and short stories, fantasy, descriptive poems, narrative poems, lyric poems or drama. The targets of attack can be as varied as religious beliefs, criminal behaviour, political institutions, or literary fashions. The emotions aroused can range from fierce indignation to mocking laughter.

In our own times, films, TV comedy shows and newspaper political cartoons attack their chosen targets. In the 18th century, satire was a prominent aspect of British literature, perhaps because the spirit of the times demanded conformity to a polished and rational norm.

The ode

The ode was one of the classical genres of lyric poetry recognised by the ancient Greeks and Romans. It involved an address to someone or something and contained lofty sentiments and thoughts. It showed a marked formality of tone and style.

'To Stella', 'Ode to Evening', 'Ode to Simplicity', 'To Spring', 'To Hope', 'To the Muses' – These are the titles of some eighteenth-century odes. (See a stanza from one of Burns's poems in this style on page 183.) Burns knew that most of his readers would expect an ode to be of that kind.

The epic

The concept of the epic poem was fixed for readers of Burns's time by the works of the legendary Greek poet Homer (about eighth century BC) and the Roman poet Virgil (70–19 BC). Alexander Pope's translations of *The Iliad* and *The Odyssey* by Homer (see page 154) showed the epic form dealing with epoch-making events of long ago and great deeds performed by heroic figures. Pope's choice of language created a tone of nobility and highmindedness. It is very tempting to make use of features of such a dignified style to make fun of less important matters.

Poetic diction

Throughout the decades previous to Burns's time, serious poetry writing had been dominated by a style largely typified by the kind of language used in the epic. Poetry of that kind was considered to be the highest form of literature, dealing with the most serious subjects in the most sublime language. Serious poetry was set apart from other kinds of writing, with distinct forms of expression: a special poetic diction. Learned and literary vocabulary, often of Latin derivation, became the expected medium for serious poetry.

Conversely, it was felt that poetry should not use commonplace or 'vulgar' language. This meant that when poets had occasion to mention the ordinary things of life, a refined and elevated form of language had to be found. One poet referred to a spade as a:

> *Metallic blade, wedded to ligneous rod,*
> *Wherewith the rustic swain upturns the sod.*

Another referred to sheep as *The bleating Kind*. These are extreme examples of circumlocution, the result of trying to avoid ordinary language by inventing a way round it.

General observations were considered more important than detailed particular instances. This influenced the way descriptions were written (e.g. pages 37–39, lines 55–90). It also resulted in the frequent use of generalisations, abstractions and the person-ification of these abstractions, as in Gray's 'Elegy' (page 140) and in parts of 'The Cotter's Saturday Night'. At its best, this style can be reflective, philosophical, dignified, seeming to rise above personal feeling or idiosyncrasy. Misapplied, it can seem artificial, deadening, pretentious.

Burns's way of life and his approach to poetry writing were at odds with much of this thinking but he could not avoid being influenced by it.

The dramatic monologue

It is never safe to assume that when a poem includes the words 'I' or 'me' the poet is sincerely expressing his or her own feelings. There is always the possibility that the poet is playing a role, assuming a persona. In a dramatic monologue the identity of the speaker is established beyond doubt as a 'character' who is not the poet. The art of the poet consists in revealing the character's personality through the character's own words.

✦ *Activities*

1   Suppose you were to reorganise this anthology under new headings such as Odes, Satires, Dramatic Monologues, The Epic, etc. Devise other headings if you think they are needed. Which poems would you place under each heading? Do some poems fit under more than one heading, or perhaps none?

2   Pick out the poems in which Burns attacks something and analyse how he sets about it in each case.

3   Here are some finer points of the poet's art which you might find in a dramatic monologue:
    • making the speaker unconsciously reveal defects of character;
    • placing the speaker in a specific dramatic situation;
    • identifying the person to whom he or she is speaking.
    Decide which of Burns's first person ('I') poems are clearly dramatic monologues. Work out which contain some of the finer points listed above.

4   Read the extracts from the poets James Beattie and Thomas Gray on pages 133 and 140 and the parts of 'The Cotter's

Saturday Night' where you can see elements of poetic diction being used. You might also find traces of it in other poems such as 'Love and Liberty', 'Scots, wha hae', and 'For a' that and a' that'. Discuss what Burns's poetry has gained or lost from the influence of this style.

5 Write a short article for your fellow students indicating the extent to which you can see Burns building on established genres of poetry in Scots and English and the extent to which he is transforming them or reacting against them.

◆

How were the poems produced?

By Burns's own account, his first poem was a song written when he was fifteen, inspired by the favourite dance tune of a fourteen-year-old girl working beside him in the harvest field, 'Thus with me began Love and Poesy'. A simple theme fused with music and close to the experience of common people – these are recurring features of Burns's output. At first he was daunted by his lack of formal education but soon took heart from his own facility and his realisation from reading the poetry collections of Allan Ramsay (1684–1758) and the poems of Robert Fergusson (1750–1774) that Scots could be used as a literary medium. He at first rhymed 'for fun' as he himself put it. He was well known and feared for his biting tongue and he used his talent in writing poems against local people he fell out with. In this he was typical of his century, as satire was a dominant form in eighteenth-century English literature and Burns had already read widely in it. Flyting, waging wars of words, was also a traditional occupation of Scottish poets. Thus he perpetuated and adapted traditional Scottish forms but was also influenced by English poetry. His poems were circulated in manuscript among his friends and beyond. It was only later that a friend suggested publication. His lifelong practice of copying out poems for his friends has led to the survival of several variants of some poems.

Only 612 copies of his first collection, The Kilmarnock Edition of Poems, Chiefly in the Scottish Dialect, were printed in the Ayrshire town, clearly a small scale provincial venture. By far the greatest part of his best work other than 'Tam o' Shanter' and the songs had already been written, but Burns carefully selected those pieces that would appeal most widely and omitted those likely to cause offence in influential quarters. It was largely by chance that his fame reached Edinburgh and Burns was encouraged to hope for national success. The First Edinburgh Edition of 1787 was of 3000 copies and contained twenty-two new pieces. With his reputation already established, Burns was able to be less cautious in what he published. The fact that he included a Scots-English glossary and several poems in English in the Kilmarnock Edition shows his intention from the first of appealing to a non-Scots-speaking audience and he further anglicised spellings and grammatical forms in the First Edinburgh Edition.

When he had made his mark in Edinburgh and become a national figure he came under considerable pressure from the leaders of Scottish literary fashion to abandon his 'uncouth' dialect and write only in Augustan English, that is the polished and formal language of eighteenth-century poetry. He wrote from Edinburgh in 1787:

> I have the advice of some very judicious friends among
> the Literati here, but with them I sometimes find it
> necessary to claim the privilege of thinking for myself.

In another letter in the same year he wrote: 'For my part, my first ambition was, and still my strongest wish is, to please my Compeers, the rustic Inmates of the Hamlet ...' A year later, after further attempts at 'polished' verse, he wrote: 'I am sick of writing where my bosom is not strongly interested.'

There were some English poems in the Kilmarnock Edition and he wrote more later, but he cast himself in the role of 'Scotia's Bard' and all his best work is generally considered to be in Scots. His nationalist impulse led to his undertaking the great task of his later life, the rescuing and enriching of the folksong and poetry of Scotland by his contributions to the song collections edited by James Johnson and George Thomson. He took fragments of folksongs and completed them, took disreputable songs and re-cast them for polite performance, took old tunes and fitted brand new words to them. He found that he could do this best in Scots. He wrote to George Thomson, the 'fastidious' editor of one of the song collections he was contributing to:

> What pleases me, as simple & naive, disgusts you as
> ludicrous & low ... These English songs gravel me to
> death. – I have not that command of the language that
> I have of my native tongue. – In fact, I think my ideas
> are more barren in English than in Scottish.

So fully was he assimilated to the folksong tradition that it is often impossible to say what is traditional and what is his own. You can judge for yourself if you look at the fragments on page 156 and 'A red red Rose' on page 119.

Many poems were first sent in letters to friends. Some remained unpublished at his death, sometimes because they were likely to make enemies that he could not afford, or because they were politically too daring, or because they were so bawdy that even he could not own to them publicly. Most of these were collected by early 19th century editors but his famous collection of bawdy songs, *The Merry Muses of Caledonia* (see page 155), became easily available only in 1965.

✦ *Activities*

1 Consider how other immensely popular writers have produced their work and reached their public. How did Burns succeed in becoming a poet of world-wide fame in a language easily readable by only a minority in the English-speaking world?

2 Burns withheld these poems from printed publication while he lived: 'Holy Willie's Prayer', 'A Poet's Welcome to his love-begotten Daughter', 'Love and Liberty (The Jolly Beggars)'.

  Imagine that Burns is dead and these poems are now being read for the first time. Role-play the reactions of a group of people who are likely to have been offended or outraged by them, for example strict Calvinists, conventional citizens or supporters of the political establishment.

———————————— ✦ ————————————

How do these poems present their subjects?

Issues in Burns's poetry

If you try to work out Burns's standpoint on some of the issues of his time you will find it hard to pin him down. The union of Scotland and England was an established fact and already 80 years old when Burns was first publishing his poems, but to Burns it was still a live issue and his feelings about it varied (as has been the case with many Scots in the last 300 years). His religious attitudes seem also to have been complex: hostile to some forms of Christianity but conforming with the established church to the extent of regular church attendance in his family pew in St Michael's Church, Dumfries. Had he a deeper anti-religious impulse? You must decide.

There were two great political events in his lifetime: the creation of an independent state in America based on rational principles; and the outbreak of the revolution in France. The response of the British government was to re-assert the status quo as established by the 1688–1689 parliamentary supremacy. Of course, Parliament – the Lords and the Commons – was totally undemocratic in those days, representing only the small ruling class.

You can look back through Burns's works for signs of his support for reform in government and in society. In the present selection they are not explicit, but are nonetheless present.

Burns's feelings for women encompass a wide range, even as represented by this limited selection of his poems. Like all considerable poets, he is capable of assuming a persona (a dramatic role) when writing a lyric. This is most evident when he writes from a woman's viewpoint. Other lyrics draw heavily on the folk tradition and are therefore less personal. Others again can be connected with particular relationships in Burns's life.

You must decide whether the background to each poem, or indeed Burns's character as we know it from his biographers, is important in responding to his art.

✦ *Activities*

1 In 'To William Simpson, Ochiltree' Burns describes the kind of
poet he wants to be. Summarise what he tells you. Compare
this with the kind of poet you know Burns to have been as a
result of reading all the poems in this selection.

2 Re-read 'The Twa Dogs', 'Life and Liberty', 'To a Louse', 'The
Cotter's Saturday Night' and 'For a' that and a' that'. How
much social change is Burns advocating? What seems to be his
social 'message'?

3 Re-read the poems in this selection which deal with aspects of
love. Compare the ways in which these poems portray
different attitudes and feelings about love.

4 Find passages in Burns's poetry which you think might
confirm the opinion that Burns uses 'the vivid concrete terms
of ordinary experience' to convey 'a universal truth' (see page
163).

5 Divide the class into groups, one group for each aspect of
Burns's life. (Decide for yourselves what these are.) Each group
is to collect quotations from the poems referring to the topic it
has been allocated and arrange them in two contrasting
columns. They should be entered on sheets of paper or card in
suitably large and varied lettering and formed into a wall
display.

Rhyme, metre and rhythm

Most of Burns's poetry is divided into stanzas and, like most
pre-twentieth-century poetry, it is written in regular metres. If a
poem is written in stanzas the rhyme scheme is repeated in each
stanza and this is one way each stanza is given its shape. Each line
forms a unit of the metre. This is why it is printed as a separate
line. It may or may not be marked off by a rhyming word at its
end.

Poetry of this period has a regular number of light and heavy
stresses in each line, arranged in a number of repeating units
called feet. A foot is a number of light and heavy stressed syllables

arranged in a pattern. For example, *They reel'd* is a light stress followed by a heavy stress.

$$x \quad / \quad x \quad / \quad x \quad / \quad x \quad /$$
They reel'd, they set, they cross'd, they cleekit

consists of four feet, each containing a light stress followed by a heavy stress. (Note the extra final syllable.)

Thus the metre of a poem written in stanzas could be thought of as being built out of three sizes of repeating patterned unit:

• stanzas;
• each stanza built out of a set number of lines;
• each line built out of a set number of feet;
• each foot consisting of a set pattern of lightly and heavily stressed syllables.

A syllable is the shortest stretch of spoken language.

You will have noticed that some of Burns's poems like 'The Twa Dogs' and 'Tam o' Shanter' are written in verse paragraphs formed from a variable number of rhyming couplets.

The commonest foot in English (and Scots) poetry is the iambus: a light stress followed by a heavy one, as in the word *behind*. (Of course, there are several other kinds of foot.) A line of poetry using iambic feet might be described as iambic pentameter (five iambic feet), or iambic tetrameter (four iambic feet). In Burns you can also find lines containing two heavy stresses (dimeter), three heavy stresses (trimeter), or occasionally even six heavy stresses (hexameter).

Of course, once you have determined the underlying metre of a poem you have only scratched the surface of the poet's art. Even although two lines conform to the same regular metre they may be different in rhythm. Rhythm is the actual movement of the poetry when it is spoken with attention to the sense of it. A comparison with music might help you to grasp the difference between metre and rhythm. Metre is like a theme tune which a musician could play over and over again. Rhythm is like the variations which might be superimposed on the underlying theme to create variety. You must read a poem aloud expressively in order to sense the variations in its rhythm. If you read it with exaggerated heavy stresses you will emphasise only the metre. When you read a poem with attention to the sense and feeling, you will reveal how its rhythm is a constant series of variations on its underlying metre.

✦ *Activities*

1 'Tam o' Shanter' would be a good example to experiment with in reading aloud. Although each line is a constant four feet consisting of a light followed by a heavy stress (with an occasional additional light stress thrown in), it would be wrong to read the poem throughout at the same pace or always bringing out these four heavy stresses. Notice also how the breaks in the sense, the phrases, create units of meaning that cut across the regular metrical pattern. Sometimes also (in other poems) the sense runs on from one line to another without a pause. This too helps to create variety and flexibility.

2 Re-read some of the poems aloud and pick out some good examples of how Burns has varied the speaking rhythm of the poetry against the regular metre in order to create effects which suit the sense.

3 Get hold of music for some of the songs. It is probably enough if you just pick out the melody and sing it. Or you could listen to a recording. Discuss how the music enhances the poetry.

Notes on some stanza forms

Standard Habbie

This stanza has an ancient ancestry in medieval Provençal and English poetry. Sometimes called Burns stanza, it was much used by Burns and other Scottish poets. The name goes back to 'The Epitaph of Habbie Simson, the piper of Kilbarchan', by Sir Robert Semple, Laird of Beltrees (c1595–c1668). Allan Ramsay called it Standard Habbie because he saw it as a standard form for Scottish poets.

The first three lines and the fifth are tetrameter (four heavy stresses); the two short lines are dimeter (two heavy stresses), all based on the iambic foot (see pages 178–179). Its characteristic feature is the short line at the end, the 'bob wheel', which, as the critic David Murison says, lends itself to the 'sardonic afterthought or phrase of finality'. The stanza is not often used for narrative but rather for poetry in a conversational style, especially for witty or humorous comment on life, as in 'To William Simpson, Ochiltree', on page 33.

Spenserian stanza: *The Cotter's Saturday Night*

Spenserian stanza is so called from its use by the Elizabethan English poet Edmund Spenser in his long allegorical romance *The Faerie Queen* (1596). Spenser's poem depicted the deeds of knights in far off days and used language already archaic in his time. Subsequent poets' use of the Spenserian stanza associated it with an archaic and magnificent style of language, lofty thoughts and aspiring sentiments. It was a popular verse form among eighteenth-century English poets for serious works, not satirical. It has eight lines of iambic pentameter (see pages 178–179) and one final iambic hexameter (six feet), rhyming ababbcbcc.

It had been used by the Scottish poets James Thomson, in 'The Castle of Indolence', and James Beattie, in 'The Minstrel', a poem much admired by Burns (see extracts on pages 132 and 133).

Tam o' Shanter

The four-beat metre is nearer to the commonest ballad metre (which has alternating four-beat and three-beat lines) than to the predominantly five-beat lines of much English verse (Shakespeare, Milton, eighteenth-century blank verse). How does the shortness of the line suit the telling of this particular tale?

The songs

These vary in the length of their lines and their rhyme schemes but use iambic feet. Have a look at 'Scots, wha hae'. How many heavy stresses are there in each line? How would you characterise the rhythm? How does this stanza suit the dramatic occasion in the poem?

✦ *Activities*

1 Write your own satire (see page 170) using the Burns stanza. Look at its technical features on page 180 under the heading of Standard Habbie. Choose a subject from your own life – a person or group you don't like, an institution or way of doing things you want to change or abolish. Are you going to use witty abuse or ridicule? Can you find the clinching phrase to fit into the 'bob wheel' at the end of each stanza?

2 Write a serious and dignified stanza in Spenserian form. Look at its technical features on page 181. You might choose to celebrate your own country, something to do with your religion, or some hero or group of heroes that everyone in your country admires. Can you use some of the language features which Burns used to dignify his poetry? (See page 171 under Poetic Diction.)

Imagery and choice of language

✦ *Activities*

1 The imagery is the sense impressions conveyed by the poems, largely, but by no means entirely, by the metaphors and similes. Identify the main aspects of human experience from which Burns drew his images.

2 Select two or three poems in which you think Burns uses a wide range of levels of language in both Scots and English. Explain what he achieves by this.

✦

Who reads these poems and how do they interpret them?

Contemporary critical reactions

Early critics recognised Burns's genius, but he was an awkward figure to fit into the literary ideas of the time. Even in Scotland, the arbiters of taste assumed that English was the proper language of literature, though they themselves used Scots as an everyday language. In typical eighteenth-century fashion, they sought 'purity', 'correctness' and 'refinement' in language. They praised Burns's poetry but were embarrassed at the fact that he wrote in dialect. They urged him to adopt the language of polished literary culture and to attempt the 'higher' literary forms such as tragedy.

Edinburgh-based critic Henry Mackenzie (well known to historians of English literature as the author of the novel *The Man of Feeling*) wrote the most influential early comment in his periodical *The Lounger* in 1786. His preconceptions about poetry led him to emphasise only certain aspects of the poems: their 'high tone of feeling', their inspiration 'solemn and sublime, with that rapt and inspired melancholy in which the poet lifts his eye above this visible diurnal sphere'. So you won't be surprised that the first four poems that he mentioned are now regarded as poor specimens of Burns's work. For instance, here is the first stanza of 'Despondency, an Ode' (You might compare this with 'To a Mouse'.)

Oppress'd with grief, oppress'd with care,
A burden more than I can bear,
*   I set me down and sigh:*
O Life! Thou art a galling load,
Along a rough, a weary road,
*   To wretches such as I!*
Dim-backward as I cast my view,
*   What sick'ning Scenes appear!*
What Sorrows yet may pierce me thro',
*   Too justly I may fear!*
*   Still caring, despairing,*
*   Must be my bitter doom;*
*   My woes here, shall close ne'er,*
*   But with the closing tomb!*

In common with a succession of later critics, he also admired 'The Cotter's Saturday Night', considering it 'tender and moral'. Early critics often quoted stanza IX, partly because its freedom from dialect recommended it to English readers.

In the second half of the eighteenth century there was a cultural movement towards admiration of the simple rural life, the primitive, 'the noble savage' (see page 166). Mackenzie accordingly described Burns as 'this Heaven-taught ploughman from his humble unlettered station'. He assumed that an Ayrshire farmer who mostly wrote in his local language must lack all education and sophistication. This was a long-standing misconception not corrected even by the comments of the London-based Scot John Logan in his *English Review* of 1787: '[In the poems] ... we can trace imitations of almost every English author of celebrity.' 'He is better acquainted with the English poets than most English authors that have come under our review.' So you should be on your guard against claims, made even by Burns himself, that he was only a simple country fellow.

Mackenzie also first voiced a continuing concern, that the poems 'breathe a spirit of libertinism and irreligion'. He regretted 'that delicacy should be so often offended'. Yet in Burns's lifetime his poetry was known and admired throughout Britain, Canada and the USA.

After Burns's death, the widely reprinted obituary notice by the song publisher George Thomson (who had never met him) fuelled gossip about his private life, in particular that he drank himself to death (refuted by modern research):

> Probably he was not qualified to fill a superior station
> to that which was assigned to him. We know that his
> manners refused to partake the polish of genteel
> society, that his talents were often obscured and finally
> impaired by excess.

This moral disapproval and class prejudice combined with distrust of Burns's known radical politics and resulted in the emergence of a current of opinion hostile to the poetry as well as to the man's memory. Yet people such as the poet William Wordsworth (1770–1850) wished to attend only to the poetry.

Writing about authors, and Burns in particular, he said, 'Our business is with their books, – to understand and to enjoy them.'

The growth of the Burns myth

Burns Clubs were founded and Burns Suppers were celebrated from early in the nineteenth century and his elevation into an icon of Scottish culture was fully accomplished by mid century. Throughout the Empire, many Scots who took no other interest in poetry read and admired his work. The appeal of his poetry can be partly ascribed to the uprooting of so many Scots from their rural background and their transfer to industrial towns in Britain or their settlement in the colonies. This process was accompanied by the further weakening of distinctively Scottish culture by English influences. Perhaps you yourself belong to a culture which feels itself undermined and weakened by an outside influence. If so, you may understand the situation in Scotland better. Burns's poetry nourished nostalgic memories of rural life and the past importance of the Scots language. Burns the lover, the reveller, the patriot, the rebel, became a national hero, as much for his personality as his poetry. The Scottish poet Edwin Muir commented on this phenomenon in 1947:

> For a Scotsman to see Burns simply as a poet is
> well-nigh an impossibility. Burns is so deeply
> embedded in Scottish life that he cannot be detached
> from it, from what is best in it and what is worst in it,
> and regarded as [we regard other Scottish writers]. He
> is more a personage to us than a poet, more a
> figurehead than a personage, and more a myth than a
> figurehead ... here is a poet for everybody, a poet who
> has such an insight into ordinary thoughts and feelings
> that he can catch them and give them poetic shape, as
> those who merely think or feel them cannot. This was
> Burns's supreme art ... it predestined him to become
> the Rabbie of Burns Nights. When we consider Burns
> we therefore include the Burns Nights with him ...They
> are his reward or punishment (whichever the fastidious
> reader may prefer to call it) for having had the temerity
> to express the ordinary feelings of his people, and
> having become a part of their life.

Yet all the major nineteenth-century English literary figures also read Burns, commented on his work and acknowledged his genius. His poems were translated into all the major European languages in the course of the nineteenth century, into Japanese in 1906 and into Russian in 1924. He was promoted by the Soviets as an advocate for the oppressed, like Charles Dickens. In the last 100 years, the most important critical and biographical studies have come from France, Germany and the USA as well as Scotland.

Modern responses to Burns

Writing an influential history of 'English' literature in the 1920s, the French critic Louis Cazamian was concerned with Burns's place in the evolution of literary styles:

> The quality of the work of Burns is that of a superior 'classicism', in the aesthetic sense of the term; ... [his art] is more an art of the intellect than of the emotions. Yet it is in close touch with all the human element in life. Compared with it the rational poetry of a Pope is dry reading. In the work of Burns are to be found the inner elements of Romanticism: personal effusion, sensibility, a keen love for nature, a wealth of imaginative fancy, a sympathetic interest in the poor and in animals.

Mid-century Scottish literary critics such as David Daiches and Thomas Crawford concentrated on his artistic achievement rather than the continuing controversies about his life. Daiches (1950) valued the satires, the verse letters and the songs. He saw him as the poet of friendship and sexual love. It is his 'high technical skill' which makes his work live. 'It is not the profundity of the philosophy but the ability to recapture the experience that is so remarkable.' His poetry is seen as essentially simple and direct: 'a kind of literature that seems to by-pass literature'. As a result, 'the most fashionable critical tools seem inappropriate in discussing his poetry'.

Crawford (1960) saw Burns as the poet of contradictions and conflicts within the individual and in society. He asserted the worth of the individual and the individual's right to freedom of opinion and action, but also wished a society based on fraternal relations:

> A ... theme to which Burns returned again and again was the uniqueness and sanctity of individual human beings – a spontaneous and passionate democratic humanism which extends to the whole of society the values of the family.
> [Another] major characteristic of Burns's was his cult of the 'Honest man', which was a common concept of the Enlightenment all over Europe ... For Burns, one feels, the ideal society was composed of independent tenant-farmers and the owners of one-man businesses.

In spite of Burns's individualism, Crawford thought he was very much an eighteenth-century poet, not a Pre-Romantic. He was 'the poet of the great commonplaces' and therein lies his universal appeal. The post-war folksong revival focussed attention on the songs, and Crawford wrote of Burns operating on 'the boundaries between poetry and music where language fuses with melody'. In this art Crawford saw him foreshadowing and equalling later song writers and folksong collectors such as Schubert, Wolf, Stravinsky and Bartok.

The American critic Carol McGuirk (1985) was concerned to rescue Burns from relegation to the status of national poet, of interest to Scots only:

> I believe that if Burns is to be reconstituted as a major poet it will not be by stressing his excellence in the use of dialect, but by showing how his work (including his poetry in dialect) does at its best achieve the classical standard of universality ... Burns combines dialect with neo-classical English, local with cosmopolitan references, in virtually all his writings to ensure effects that transcend narrow 'particularity' ... Dialect and all,

> Burns in fact meets one of the best established criteria
> for classic literary stature. In Longinus's words: 'You
> should consider that to be truly beautiful and sublime
> which pleases all people at all times.'

She also refuted the view that Burns had very little 'visionary imagination' of the kind that creates a whole mythical world such as the 'world' of Thomas Hardy or William Faulkner (to name two artists who have strong regional associations).

> ... surely the 'Scotland' [of Burns] is as much an
> invented world as those of Hardy, Faulkner ... It is a
> sign of Burns's success that his world seems 'real' and
> 'natural'.

Kenneth Simpson (1988) emphasised that the Burns 'cult' actually damages the reputation of Burns the poet:

> Now because certain of the poems originate in the
> poet's own moods and experiences many devotees
> assume this of virtually all the poems and read them
> literally ... However one effect of the Burns cult is to
> close minds to awareness of any self-irony in Burns's
> poems and to respond, not to a *persona*, but to the
> 'true' voice of the poet. In fact, far from being records
> of actual experience, many of Burns's poems render
> experiences which are the creation of the imagination.
> In Burns, those energies which might have led to the
> writing of plays were channelled instead into his
> poems, his conversation, and his behaviour.

And still mountains of haggis are consumed annually by people of all ranks at Burns Suppers throughout the world, with their uncanny resemblance to the ritual of the Mass: the ceremonial entry of the haggis, the reciting of the 'Address to the Haggis' while it is slit open, its distribution and eating, the prescribed speeches: 'To the Lassies', 'The Reply to the Lassies', 'The Immortal Memory' – emotional protestations of devotion to an only partly understood hero. The biography-writing industry continues apace, now proposing to exhume the Bard's corpse to take DNA samples from it in an attempt to establish the paternity of a possible child of Highland Mary, one of the poet's 'lady friends'. And still his face is reproduced on thousands of shortbread tins, teatowels and other tourist trumpery. And still hundreds of thousands of ordinary people throughout the world can quote his poetry although they read no other.

◆ Activities

1 It is 26 January, the day after Burns's birthday and the innumerable Burns Suppers held the world over. Your local newspaper contains a lengthy report of the fulsome speech made at the local Burns Club to 'The Immortal Memory of Robert Burns'. Write a letter to the Editor in which you complain about 'Bardolatry'. Now write the reply from another reader a few days later.

2 It is late in 1786 and Burns has reached Edinburgh on his borrowed pony. His fame has gone before him, Henry Mackenzie's review of the Kilmarnock poems has been published and Burns is received in the great houses of the capital. Burns is in conversation with Mackenzie and some of the other leaders of literary fashion. They are urging on him their view of the kind of poetry he should now write. He replies in detail, justifying his intentions partly by referring to his past work. Stage the discussion, each taking a role.

3 If you are a Scot, consider to what extent your Scottishness prejudices you unjustifiably in favour of Burns's poetry. Or does your Scottish background actually help you to comprehend Burns's attitudes and values?
OR
If you are a non-Scot, consider to what extent you find Burns's poetry either universal or rather limited in its appeal. Account for your findings by considering not only its Scots language but also its attitudes and values.

4 Burns lived and died more than 200 years ago. What did Burns value and celebrate which you too, who live in the modern

world, can value and celebrate? You could mount a debate on a suitable motion.

5   In groups, explore the reasons why Burns is so popular with ordinary non-poetry readers throughout the world.

———————————————— ◆ ————————————————

FURTHER READING

Poems and letters

Rhymer Rab, An Anthology of Poems and Prose by Robert Burns (ed. Bold) (Black Swan, 1993) Contains a note to each poem giving background and origins; useful introductory material; a good selection of letters; a glossary.
ISBN 0 552 99526 6

The Burns Federation Song Book (ed. McVie) (The Burns Federation, Dick Institute, Elmbank Avenue, Kilmarnock KA1 3BU, Scotland.) Simple arrangements of 20 songs: 'Scots, wha hae'; 'Is there for honest poverty'; 'A red, red Rose'; 'O, wert thou in the cauld blast'; 'Auld lang syne'.

Burns: Poems and Songs (ed. Kinsley) The complete poetic works, with the melodic line for each song. (Oxford, 1992)
ISBN 0 19 281114 2

Criticism and biography

A. Bold, *A Burns Companion* (Macmillan, 1991)
A handbook containing articles on the main aspects of Burns's background – language, religion, politics, booze, bawdy – and all the main poems individually.
ISBN 0 333 42270 8

T. Crawford, *Burns, a Study of the Poems and Songs* (Canongate, 1994) A literary study, with helpful analysis of all the major works, notice taken of the linguistic background and a special appendix on pronunciation.
ISBN 0 898410 14 3

D. Daiches, *Robert Burns* (Spurbooks, Holmes McDougall, 1981) Probably the best recent full-length literary study, relating Burns clearly to the Scots literary tradition.
ISBN 0 7157 2093 7

I. Grimble, *Robert Burns* (Lomond Books, 1994)
A no-nonsense version of Burns's life and personality, with a slightly different viewpoint by a Gaelic-speaking Scot. Many

excellent illustrations conveying the physical conditions of Burns's life. ISBN 1 85152 734 6

W. Kay, *Scots – The Mither Tongue* (Grafton Books, 1988) A detailed account of the evolution of the Scots language up to the present day. ISBN 0 586 20033 9

K. Simpson, *Robert Burns* (Scotnotes No 9) (Association for Scottish Literary Studies, 1994) A short literary study of the most important poems. Intended for senior school students. ISBN 0 948877 22 7

Recordings

Scotsoun, 13 Ashton Road, Glasgow G12 8SP, Scotland.
Poems Chiefly in the Scottish Dialect
Poems of Robert Burns, Vols 1–3 (tape cassettes)

Association for Scottish Literary Studies, c/o Dept of English, University of Aberdeen, Aberdeen AB9 2UB, Scotland.
Three Poems of Burns (tape cassette) by Prof R. D. S. Jack ('Tam o' Shanter'; 'John Anderson my Jo'; 'Holy Willie's Prayer'). Readings, singing and commentary.

Lismor Recordings, 27–29 Carnoustie Place, Glasgow G5 8PH, Scotland.
The Robert Burns Collection: The Words. Includes 'A red red Rose'; 'Holy Willie's Prayer'; 'The Cotter's Saturday Night'; 'Tam o' Shanter'; 'To a Mouse'; 'The Twa Dogs'; 'To a Louse'; 'Ae fond kiss'; 'Auld lang syne'. Superb readings by Tom Fleming. (1995) CD. LCOM 6042.
The Robert Burns Collection: The Songs. Includes 'A man's a man'; 'A red red Rose'; 'Ae fond kiss'; 'Scots, wha hae'; 'John Anderson my Jo'; 'Auld lang syne'. A variety of styles but always good. (1995) CD. LCOM 6040.